Allen & Unwin
83 Alexander Street
Crows Nest NSW 2065
Australia

Phone: (61 2) 8425 0100
Fax: (61 2) 9906 2218
Email: info@allenandunwin.com
Web: www.allenandunwin.com

Cataloguing-in-Publication data is available from the National Library of Australia.

ISBN 978 1 74175 376 9.

Concept: Anthea Paul
Photography: copyright © Anthea Paul / Girlosophy Pty Limited
Graphic design: Charlie Birks, Sally Fahey / Happy Families Design
Illustrations & artwork: Charlie Birks, Sally Fahey /
                         Happy Families Design

Cover design: Charlie Birks, Sally Fahey / Happy Families Design
Cover photography: copyright © Anthea Paul / Girlosophy Pty Limited
Additional cover artwork: Lisa White

Other photos: pp.34-5, 68-9, 94-5, 119, 130-1, 141, 164-5: istockphoto; p.54: courtesy Lizzie Nunn; pp.70-1 & 170-1: courtesy Nina Haase; p.88-9: courtesy Romy Campbell Hicks; p.115: Happy Families; pp.146-7: courtesy Joni Caminos; pp.148-9: courtesy Simone King; p.153: courtesy Zoe Birks; p.158: Sally Fahey; p.167 main pic: Drew Brown; pp.168-9: courtesy Jess Mignone; p.174: Happy Families; pp.201-3: Charlie Birks & Sally Fahey; p.208 bottom right pic: Happy Families; pp. 220-1: Louis Birks.

Anthea Paul wishes to thank all who contributed images to this project.

Printed in China by Everbest Printing Co., Ltd

10 9 8 7 6 5 4 3 2 1

THE GIRLO TRAVEL SURVIVAL KIT

anthea paul

ALLEN&UNWIN

FOR PAPPA
6TH JUNE, 2007

CONTENTS

"ALONE I WANDER A **THOUSAND** MILES. AND I ASK MY WAY FROM THE **WHITE CLOUDS.**

TIBETAN BUDDHIST PROVERB"

Welcome to The Girlo Travel Survival Kit, the eighth book in the girlosophy series. It's been quite a journey! This book is a direct outcome of many trips taken over the years, and has certainly been a long time coming. Many air, land and sea miles have added up to a lot of notes – in my head mostly – and it felt like the right time to bring them all together in a neat, portable package, for those girlosophers who have the wanderlust.

For some of us, just getting up the courage to imagine being able to **take off to distant shores or greener pastures** is a hurdle in itself. However, it is my firm belief that life is a lot more fun when there are things to look forward to. Saying goodbye to friends and family at the airport constantly can be, like, so last year. If you can relate to that statement, something has to change. Whether you're in the midst of exams or a breakup, working under the gun, or just wishing there was a holiday somewhere on the horizon, **the sooner you start planning, the better!**

Probably the most popular travel excursion these days is the good old 'Gap Year'. It has become a rite of passage for school leavers. It's a great way to really change gears and use the year between finishing high school and going to college or university. Taking off into the unknown with your Bestie or by yourself for a year is a delicious prospect, and one that never loses its allure. For some adventurous souls it becomes a permanent way of life – love, work or a 'calling' intervenes – and they find themselves living in another country for good.

If life is all about your options, then it must be said (if rather confusingly) that options tend to reveal themselves when you are open to them doing so. And traveling is one way to discover just what these may be for you. Sometimes all it takes is a trip to fling **open the doors**. I truly hope **this book inspires you** to explore options and **create new life choices**, and to develop the courage to step through such new doorways.

Travel is a great and exciting topic although, it must be said, one that is truly massive and there are many versions of how you can travel. The old chestnut – that you can't take everything with you – still stands the test of time and so from these pages, what I call my **basic travel kit**, you will eventually have to decide for yourself what will make it onto your personal list of essentials.

As any experienced traveler will tell you, travel rarely goes exactly according to plans. But then again, if everything was completely smooth and predictable, there wouldn't be much to look forward to. Much less to talk about afterwards! You need stories to swap over the campfire at the end of your Milford Sound trek. Or, on the bow of the boat while you're crossing the Pacific. Or to help tick off the miles passing under the wheels of the train from your railway sleeper bed as you cross the desert in Rajasthan. You get the idea.

Even if it's a family holiday you're going on, you can still prepare for the trip and approach the experience as if you were doing it on your own. **You can have amazing experiences no matter what.** Travel is about the stuff you didn't expect to find as well as what you hoped for. Often the things that stay with you are not the over-photographed iconic tourist destinations that are the fodder of most guide books, but the quirky, crazy things that happened or what you saw or did along the way.

Perhaps the best thing about taking a trip is the people you met and talked with, or shared meals and moments with. One of my best travel memories involves a fabulous taxi driver in South Africa who got me to a rescheduled flight on time even though we stopped on the road for at least 20 minutes at sunrise to watch about 17 chimpanzees (ranging from adults to babies!) cross the road directly in front of the car.

NOW THAT'S GOLD.

A common misconception about traveling is that it costs too much. It's true, travel can be expensive, but with a bit of research and some careful penny pinching, it needn't be. **Travel does not necessarily mean long-distance flights and/or expensive luxury cruises. Travel can be by bike, walk, kayak, horseback trek, camel adventure or any number of options.** Even the good old family car! One of the reasons why I love car trips is that in terms of the number of people you travel with, they are intimate experiences. Going on holidays by car can be among the most hilarious times you ever have. And this is the ultimate cliché about traveling of course, but

GETTING THERE USUALLY IS HALF THE FUN.
IT CAN EVEN BE MOST OF THE FUN IF YOU HAVE
<u>THE RIGHT ATTITUDE.</u>

Except, of course, when it goes all pear-shaped and you find yourself in the midst of drama half a world away from everyone or anyone who could possibly help. I'll get back to this later!

And so we come to the nub of it. Why do we desire to leave the comfort of what we know? Why do we 'up and leave' (if only temporarily) our friends and family, beloved pets, our routine, our own room – our own comfortable bed! – and head off into the frequently uncomfortable, often unpredictable and sometimes downright unbearable, unknown? Put simply, curiosity: that healthy sense of wanting to see what else is actually 'Out There'. At a certain level, I believe it's also the knowledge that we can't control everything and … the sneaking suspicion that it might actually be fun not to.

WHEN YOU TRAVEL,
YOU QUICKLY LEARN TO EXPECT THE UNEXPECTED.

Ultimately, **no matter what kind of trip you have**, **travel is always an education**. To me, the experience of traveling is the same as putting yourself into an accelerated learning scenario. You're frequently in the dark and more often than not you have to work it out on your own.

In considering what might be helpful, I have created seven sections in the book to assist you:

1. inspiration –
   where to go,
   how to choose a destination

2. Planning –
   Lists, reminders,
   eye-openers, pitfalls

3. Preparation –
   baggage, packing, training

4. Departures –
   final check-lists, leaving home,
   fond farewells

5. in transit –
   what to wear, security,
   getting into travel mode

6. on the road –
   travel tips, general stuff

7. coming home –
   adjusting, new routines,
   what to expect.

This book is my nutshell version of the crucial travel must-haves, must-sees, and must-dos before, during and after your trip. In the back section of **The Girlo Travel Survival Kit** I have included a trip planner, a basic budgeting section, portable (purpose-specific!) address book and a few extras to keep in mind while you're out there in the world! It will hopefully be your constant inspiration for many journeys to come. There's no need to be afraid: **girlo will be with you**!

The planet is still the same size as it has always been, but it's never been more available to see. Here's a little known fact: there aren't actually thousands of hard and fast rules when it comes to traveling. There are a few tips and a few rules, well more than a few maybe, but there are – confusingly – almost always exceptions. The trick is to know when the exceptions apply and how best to look out for them.

The thing about travel is that it is an intensely personal experience. You may take the exact same package tour as another friend or group of friends but this has no bearing on how you will each perceive it. That's why you should only take suggestions from people about things like accommodation and food if they actually share your tastes. But – and here's an exception to that rule! – the pay-off in taking a chance is more often than not a positive one. It could be amazing either way: good or bad. The whole point is there is a degree of risk in anything you do, but you have to listen to your gut instinct and trust it to minimize any downsides. You just have to have a go. **You need to be open to the experience** whatever it is.

AT ITS CORE, TRAVELING IS ABOUT DECISION-MAKING. YOU HAVE TO BE WILLING TO LIVE WITH THE CONSEQUENCES OF A DECISION.

And that is why travel is not for the fainthearted.

One of the least discussed aspects of traveling is that how you travel is very often mirrored by how you are feeling in your own skin at the time, yet magnified! You can't leave everything behind – any more than you can leave your problems behind – they tend to come with you and they're usually still there when you get home. This is why **traveling can be brilliant for a fresh perspective,** even if it's not necessarily a cure-all. It is unrealistic to expect a trip to change your life, although – here's another exception – it can.

Travel can be illuminating and inspiring and uplifting at best, but it can also be frustrating, disappointing and all of the things that everyday life at home can be. The things that work for one individual – as in relationships, and as in life! – may not work for anyone else. The road may be there to share. But **the code of the road is up to each person to divine for herself.**

"WHEN YOU TRAVEL IT SHOULD BE WITH A SENSE OF PURPOSE"

Some of the things I am frequently asked by girlosophy readers include where to go, what to take and how long to go for, and of course, how much one can expect it to cost. I've tried to give you as much information as I can to help you in making these decisions. More recently I am being asked about projects and **volunteering that can be done in conjunction with a trip, a wonderful altruistic approach to seeing the world** and learning about other cultures whilst helping those less fortunate at the same time. I have therefore included a few inspiring destinations with a purpose. It is my hope for all girlosophers who want to plug into this vast and extreme world of ours, that when you travel it is with a sense of purpose. **This is the way to get the most out of your wanderings**.

There is no formula for the perfect travel experience. One person's idea of paradise is another person's version of watching paint dry and yet another's experience of hell. Hence the need to know yourself! If you know yourself or you work on what it is you're expecting from the travel experience you're planning, you'll almost never have a bad time anywhere. You will always be able to find the upside, even if it all seems too hard.

Having said that, I trust that what you'll find in these pages will encourage you to dust off that atlas, drag out the world map, click on to Google Earth and start dreaming, if not actually planning and booking the trip of a lifetime ... or even a short trip to a place you have always yearned to go.

BIGGER ISN'T ALWAYS BETTER.

Lastly, it wouldn't be a girlo book if I didn't urge you in some way to **take a spiritual approach to your traveling**. Please be aware that as a visitor for any length of time, you are still a guest in your host country as much as you are an ambassador for your own and – no matter what – you should behave accordingly. I'll talk more about this in the course of the book.

My best travel tip is one that has served me more
than any other and is as follows:

"ON YOUR
JOURNEYS, TAKE THE
THEIR PEOPLE,
CUSTOMS
AND THEIR
PLACES
INTO YOUR
HEART & SOUL.
RESOLVE TO
GIVE BACK
JUST AS MUCH
AS YOU HAVE
DISCOVERED
AND YOU WILL FIND
LIMITLESS
EXPANSION THEREIN."

This is how I want you to be inspired. I always want you to be inspired! But above all I hope that yours will be an **elevated travel experience**. That's the type to aim for. Certainly I wish and hope for you that when you do come home you are brimming with enthusiasm, breathless with stories and at the same time humbled with gratitude.

Of course, none of this can actually happen if you just gaze in the window at the discount flight center. I want you to set a plan, a budget, make the booking, and to go. And please, when you get there, send me a postcard!

Wishing you many happy returns and much aloha spirit wherever in the world you may find yourself.

ANTHEA PAUL
HAWAII 2007

CHAPTER 1

INSPIRATION

I THINK I HAVE HAD MY MOST TESTING AND REWARDING TIMES TRAVELING – [BOTH] BY MYSELF AND WITH OTHERS.
I LEARNED PATIENCE IS THE KEY …

It is a bit of a wake-up call leaving your comfort zone (home) to go to another country, where you can't speak the language too well and the money, smells, food, water and transport is nothing like what you're used to.

My road rules for travel:

1. Every opportunity I get to travel, I take it!
2. Learn to be organized! You should always rely on yourself first.
3. Be safety conscious but never be rude to anyone whom you encounter; these connections may become friends (which is super handy when you're on a journey by yourself!).
4. Don't be afraid to have a go at making friends with some of the local people, only the locals know the secret spots. If you earn their respect and trust you may just luck onto a special experience. I believe every destination has a secret spot!

5. Be brave

That way you'll make the most of your traveling opportunities

CRYSTAL SIMPSON
GIRLOSOPHER & SURF GUIDE
YALLINGUP SURF SAFARIS

CRYSTAL SIMPSON
GIRLOSOPHER & SURF GUIDE

23

PAGE #

CHAPTER #

1

INSPIRATION

CHAPTER

DARE TO DREAM

The trip that takes us far away, to a place of our imaginations, is something that never fails to stir the soul in some way. The dream of travel, of leaving everything we know behind, is something that strikes us all at some point. **Where (on Earth!) have you dreamed of going?** Have you always had this desire to go there or is it something more recent? Perhaps it's been a gradual realization for you, but no matter how you come to it, a dream – which can become a true goal in itself – can take time to manifest, sometimes years, even decades. But the important thing about a dream is that however long it takes to do so, **the planning will all seem like a nanosecond once you get there**.

Take your dreams seriously because they are part of your personal mythology. **Act on your desires and be amazed by where they can take you**. You have no idea what you're capable of until you throw yourself out there. You'll be stoked by your own abilities – traveling is one of the greatest confidence builders. You could dream about taking charge of your life and do nothing about it, or you can make it happen. But the dream itself is critical because the dream begets the plan. **Your dream creates a hunger and therefore a goal**.

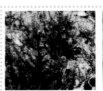

Travel is a path to personal growth. You will rarely be exactly the same at the beginning of a trip as you are at the end. A trip away will almost always change you, and it may even be life-changing. And you should be prepared for this fact.

YOUR DREAM IS TRULY YOUR PERSONAL QUEST.

CHOOSING A DESTINATION

How do you know where and when to go? Well, to start with, it should be to somewhere you have a very strong feeling about. And you shouldn't be persuaded to go somewhere because Aunt Mabel said it was the best holiday she ever had – ten years ago. Or even because a close girlfriend has a dream about some place she wants to visit – it may not work for you (especially if she's got this 'thing' that she'll meet her soulmate there!).

A destination should have a sense of ... well ... destiny about it – a destiny for you and you alone. You may well share an excitement about a destination with a friend but be sure it's for the right reasons. It will be a choice you'll have to live with, so it may as well feel right for you from the beginning.

CHOOSE WISELY AND CHOOSE WELL. NO REGRETS.

From my experience that, apart from having a strong feeling about a place, even if I may have just heard someone talking about it, there are often other **'signs'** that inspire me to visit a place or spend good amounts of time traveling there. These signs have included articles in magazines or television documentaries about a place or country, but all of a sudden (or so it has seemed) it passes within my radar. Or, the name seems to be coming up in odd ways, such as a book I may pick up and flick through will contain a reference to the place of some sort. Or I come across something completely unrelated like a profile of someone who was born there or who has some connection there. All these things can conspire to inspire. So be on the lookout for such off-beat and unexpected indicators, because you just never know. **Put them all together and it may add up to ... your personal destiny!**

TRAVELING WITH PURPOSE

VOLUNTEERING

There are many opportunities for those who wish to inject some altruism and humanity into their travel experiences. Volunteering on non-profit projects is possible in many countries. This way, you are able to connect immediately with local people (and other travelers) who are on the ground and have loads of knowledge to share, plus you'll have the satisfaction of knowing you are helping others in the process. What could be better than that?

The back section of this book, 'Traveling with the world wide web', lists some websites to get you started, if you are interested in making a real difference on your journeys.

THAT'S TRAVELING REAL GIRLO-STYLE!

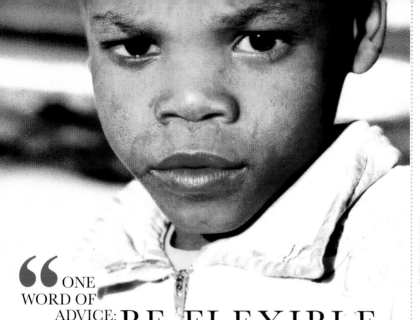

66 ONE WORD OF ADVICE; BE FLEXIBLE. 'AWAITING ANGELS' WILL ALWAYS TRY TO ACCOMODATE YOUR DESIRES, BUT YOUR VOLUNTEER WORK IS ALWAYS SUBJECT TO CHANGE. JUST HAVE FUN WITH WHATEVER YOU END UP DOING!

DON'T STRESS OUT. WORKING WITH CHILDREN IS CHALLENGING, ESPECIALLY IN ANOTHER LANGUAGE. 99

SARAH BERINGER
VOLUNTEERS ABROAD
AS QUOTED ON THE INTERNET

THINKING BECOMES OPPORTUNITY

Just imagining going on a trip can start with a sense of where you might need to go. It can be a place where you feel or know that something can be achieved in some way, even if it's just to chill out, or as a means to reconcile something within you that is unresolved. For me, this part is never something I can precisely put my finger on, but it is something I rarely feel conflicted about once I have a sense of it. I have never had a problem choosing which country or what trip to make because I have always had a clear-cut intuition that where I am heading is right for me at this particular time in my life. **If a trip neatly aligns with a sense of purpose then that's the Holy Grail**. Perhaps you have always known that Vietnam is a special place for you, that something about the place just calls you. Perhaps you just don't feel this way about a particular place at all. **Just pay attention** –

IT CAN BE MORE MEANINGFUL TO TRAVEL WITH YOUR INSTINCT

Intuition is your primary travel tool – even before you go away. If you focus on tuning in to it, you will always make good choices (that includes working out your itinerary!) or, failing that, you will be in a much better position to work out a fallback position that is appropriate and right for you. Not only that, you will never be pressured into going somewhere that isn't 'you'. For example, if you get really seasick, for goodness sake do not let yourself (against your better judgment) be talked into a Trans-Pacific crossing in a yacht!

This is especially so if you really feel anxious about any idea or unsure about it as a deep gut feeling. Likewise if you hate the cold or camping out but your Bestie wants you to go trekking in Nepal with her during winter. **Figuring out your likes and dislikes will alert you to what not to do for your own sake, not to mention your self-preservation**. At the very least you will have a long list of things to be on the lookout for when you are still in the planning stages of your trip.

> "WITHOUT NEW EXPERIENCES, SOMETHING INSIDE OF US SLEEPS. THE SLEEPER MUST AWAKEN.

FRANK HERBERT
SCIENCE FICTION AUTHOR

THINKING BECOMES OPPORTUNITY

31

INSPIRATION

DAZED AND CONFUSED?

If you truly feel that you want to travel but are equally sure you don't know where you want to go, then you have your work cut out for you. **There are many ways to become inspired by a destination.** As it is said, there are many paths to the mountain! So you'll have to be a bit more dedicated to discover what or where you are truly passionate about.

It doesn't matter how you work this stuff out, it just helps to have a process or a system of sorts to cut through the maze. You could start by simply reading novels set in specific locations as these may teach you something of interest about the culture of the place.

FAMILY TIES

Do you speak a second or third language? **You could visit the countries where your talent could be a real advantage.** That's something to work with, and it makes it easier when you're traveling to have a more meaningful connection with local people.

Perhaps you have parents who were born overseas and they can give you guidance. Perhaps they will be able to hook you up with family accommodation (even a sofa in a sunroom works for the budget!) so you can ease into travel mode and at the least learn about your family history in the process.

"LIFE
IS EITHER A
DARING ADVENTURE
OR
NOTHING
"

HELEN KELLER
DEAF AND BLIND AUTHOR AND TRAILBLAZER
A TRUE GIRLOSOPHER

TRAVEL IS AN ART FORM

Travel is like art, a profound and wonderful way to be inspired. If you're creative or looking to have a career in the creative industries you may well find or already know what art moves and uplifts you. If you visit art galleries close to home you might discover what exhibitions of interest may be on offer in other countries. These can then form part of your mission when you're traveling. **You may even be inspired to create an artwork yourself.**

ART CAN FEED PART OF YOUR SPIRIT
IN THE TRUEST SENSE AND INSPIRE YOU.

MAPPING IT OUT

Maps are wonderful, and crucial, tools for traveling. **You simply must know a bit of the geography of a place before you go anywhere!** So fire up your imagination by pulling out that old atlas at Mom and Dad's. Try a 'let your fingers do the walking' exercise, just for fun, as a warm-up.

Close your eyes, flip open the back of the atlas and move your finger down the index. Stop where you feel like it and flip to the map/location your finger landed on. Do you know that part of the world? Is it somewhere that sounds interesting, rings a bell or otherwise 'clicks' for you?

If the answer is yes, then perhaps you can take the next step and read up that locale's history or Google it. Take some notes anyway or start a file called 'My Trip Research'. **The notes you jot down could come in handy later when you're ready to book that trip.**

If it doesn't work for you the first time try the exercise again, as many times as you like. **Even if you don't feel anything concrete or conclusive, just enjoy the process of discovery.**

PICK UP THAT ATLAS AND FLICK!
YOUR TRAVEL EDUCATION HAS BEGUN.

MOVING MAGIC

Movies are fun, but here's another reason to hire that new-release DVD: **immerse yourself in the film's locations as films often inspire travel dreams**. Watch **The Bourne Identity** or **Oceans 12** and be inspired to ride your own Vespa through Italy. Feeling a bit blah about Europe (If George Clooney or Brad Pitt on Italy's Lake Como isn't motivation enough for you...)? Then what about **Out of Africa?** It has probably been the inspiration for more African safaris than any advertising campaign. For a bit of a thriller get **The Beach** – let Leo diCaprio be your inspiration to visit Thailand! And of course who doesn't adore a man with a motorbike (and cute goggles)? **The Motorcycle Diaries'** Gael Garcia Bernal should have you in South America in no time. For more gritty realism, try **City of Joy**, the heartwarming film set in India's Calcutta and be inspired Mother Theresa-style. If you think Mexico might be your thing, Salma Hayek in **Frida** will get you practicing your Spanish in no time! And of course don't forget the Big Apple – New York City – scene of countless romantic comedies. Visit Manhattan's Central Park and you may end up starring in your own romance!

DOING THE RIGHT THING

Traveling with the purpose of doing your bit to contribute to the world is surely one of the highest forms of travel. **This is travel inspiration at its purest.** **Becoming a volunteer for an NGO** (non-government organization) – a charity or a privately funded concern – is a great way to see the world and give back to it at the same time. In this case your inspiration might be guided by the type of volunteer work you can do – which may dictate where you travel to.

If you want to help with **rural or agricultural projects**, you may end up going to Southeast Asia or Africa or South America. Perhaps you want to help **rebuild communities after a tsunami or earthquake** or other natural or man-created disaster, so you will head for those areas affected by the tragedy. If **teaching children** is something you feel strongly about, then maybe you will go to South America, to Peru for instance. Or perhaps you want to **save the animals** and assist in caring for the elephants in Thailand or go help the dogs of Bali or India to live a happier, healthier life.

There are as many destinations to help out as there are vocations, so if you have a 'calling' to do something for others in this lifetime, then there is without doubt a special place for you in the world.

SPORTS GIRLOS HAVE FUN TOO

One of the simplest ways to narrow the field on travel destinations is to do it on the basis of **what you'll do once you get there**. If you're a keen snowboarder, surfer, or golfer, then you probably already have a clear travel wish list of surf breaks, ski resorts or golf courses running through your mind most of the time. Then, of course, all you'll have to do is figure out when the best weather conditions or seasons are for the best times for you to travel to them.

Perhaps you're a member of a sporting group or team. You can have tons of fun going away together – and also reap the savings benefits of a bulk booking. If you're under the legal age you'll have to have a chaperone/legal guardian, but this doesn't mean you won't have the experience of your life. **Maybe your school can organize a trip as an excursion so you can play sport against a school in another country**.

PETITION YOUR TEACHERS!

If you have always wanted to bungee jump, tandem skydive or if you like other adventure sport activities, then that means you'll probably be checking out places like New Zealand, South Africa or Australia. **Picking a destination because you can do your favorite activity there (or even one you've always wanted to try) is an obvious and easy starting point for planning a trip**. In addition, you will have lots of fun and taking pictures of your various escapades will have a huge pay-off with the memories you will have to look back on once you get home.

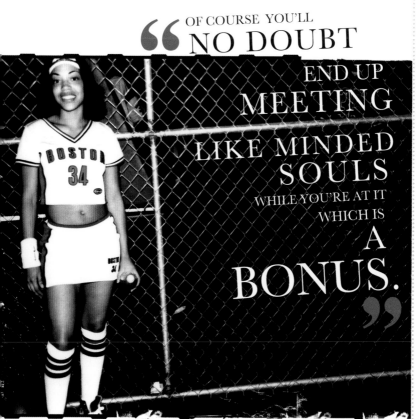

" OF COURSE YOU'LL
NO DOUBT
END UP
MEETING
LIKE MINDED
SOULS
WHILE YOU'RE AT IT
WHICH IS
A
BONUS.
"

FOREIGN EXCHANGE

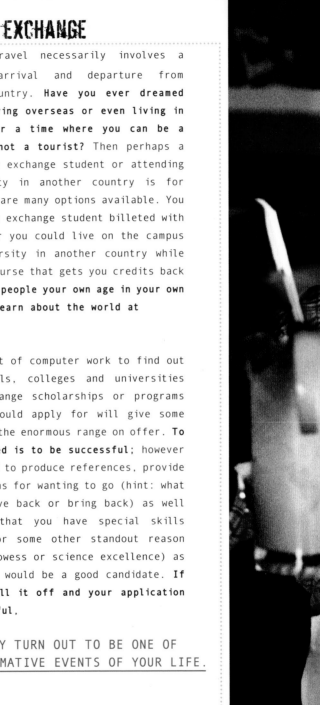

Not all travel necessarily involves a standard arrival and departure from another country. **Have you ever dreamed about studying overseas or even living in a place for a time where you can be a local and not a tourist?** Then perhaps a stint as an exchange student or attending a university in another country is for you. There are many options available. You could be an exchange student billeted with a family or you could live on the campus of a university in another country while you do a course that gets you credits back home. **Meet people your own age in your own field and learn about the world at first hand.**

A little bit of computer work to find out what schools, colleges and universities offer exchange scholarships or programs that you could apply for will give some idea as to the enormous range on offer. **To be organized is to be successful;** however you'll need to produce references, provide your reasons for wanting to go (hint: what you can give back or bring back) as well as prove that you have special skills to offer or some other standout reason (sports prowess or science excellence) as to why you would be a good candidate. **If you can pull it off and your application is successful,**

YOUR TRIP MAY TURN OUT TO BE ONE OF THE MOST FORMATIVE EVENTS OF YOUR LIFE.

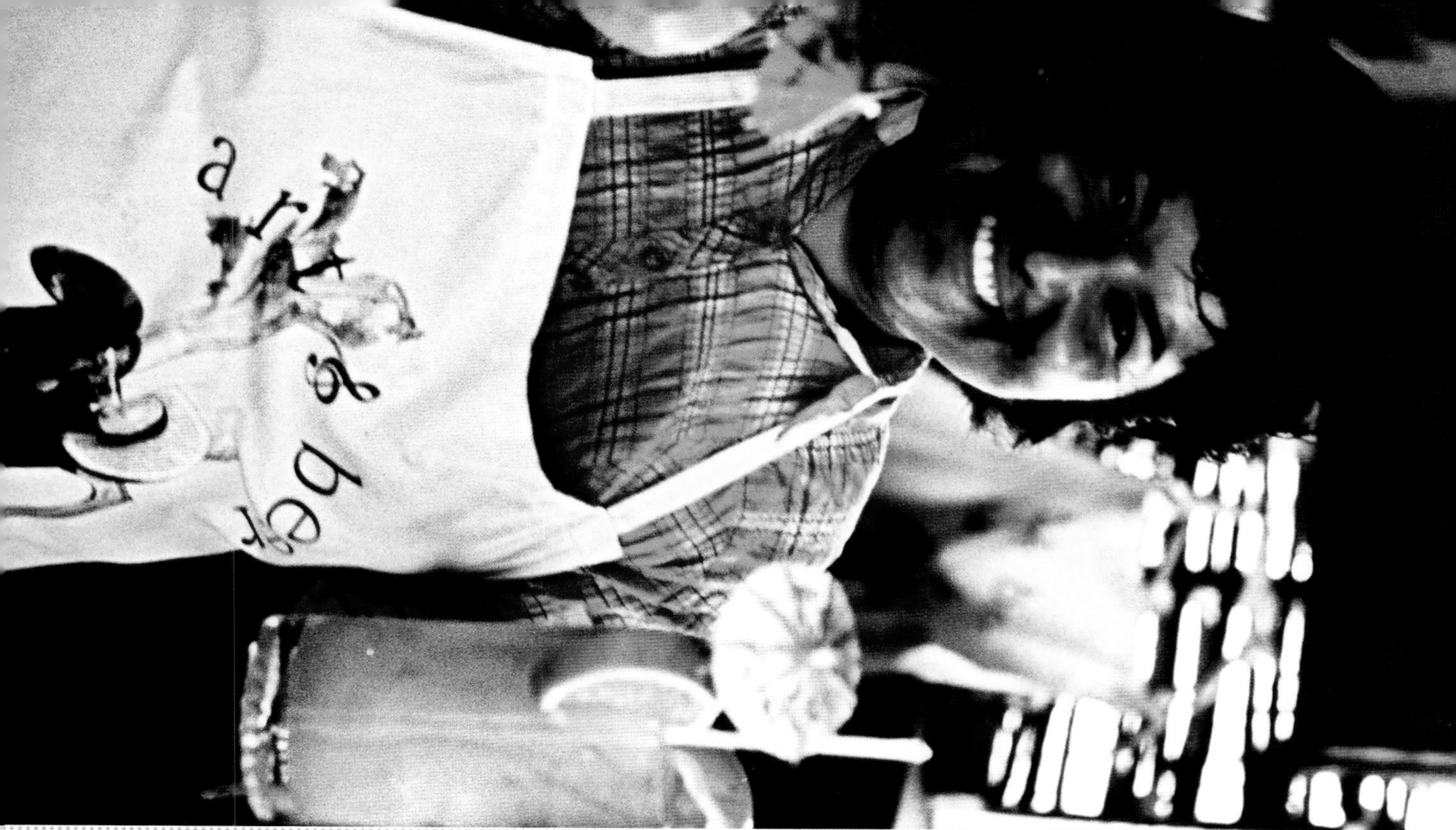

FAMILY HOLIDAYS

Traveling with the folks can be a fantastic way to see the world. Trust me on this. **When the trip is on Mom and Dad appreciate it, you'll have to pay for your own travels sooner than you think**. You may never have wanted to go to Rome or Barcelona but you can really grow from the experience of going overseas with your family as a first step to doing it by yourself later on.

A FEW RULES OF THE FAMILY TRAVEL GAME:

1. Don't begrudge parents for choosing the places you're going
   - if they pay, they get to say.
2. Be grateful, enthusiastic and join in with the planning - they
   may even ask you if there is a special thing you'd like to do.
3. Don't ever be a spoiled brat about any aspect of the traveling,

even if you have to share a room with your kid sister and she drives you crazy with her Barbie doll obsession. It's always a treat to travel. When you finally have to pay for and plan your own travels, you will soon understand what a wonderful opportunity they are offering you and how cool going away with your family can be.

4. Even if you have the odd argument (which hopefully blows over quickly) you should realize that it's all part of the deal. Arguments happen sometimes, especially when you're cooped up with people for long periods of time.

5. Remember, you will come back with a wider view of life if you look at everything as positively as you can, and take every opportunity offered – and that's very much to your personal advantage.

Offer to help with the research for the trip – you can probably Google Earth as well if not better than your parents. You can be responsible for finding out some fun activities you can all enjoy as a family. Be the one to propose certain outings. Read up on The Louvre and what Old Masters can be seen there. Be the one who knows that you need to book tickets in advance to see a show on Broadway. You'll not only be rewarded with the satisfaction of **being in charge of your own happiness**, you'll be truly empowered as a result.

Okay, so the photos that stay on the family kitchen fridge for years will almost certainly be a source of major fashion embarrassments (those weird boots you bought in Italy) and hair fiascos (why you should never ever get your hair cut on a whim at the trendiest hair salon in London), and without a doubt will feature the only skin breakout moment you had on the trip (too many chocolate croissants in Paris), but **they'll be your memories to treasure, forever**.

BE POSITIVE, BE MATURE, AND BE HELPFUL –
YOU'LL GET MORE OUT OF IT IF YOU ARE.

45

INSPIRATION

SIZE DOESN'T MATTER!

Travel comes in all forms and a weekend away can be as eye opening and amazing as a six-month epic if the elements line up. I treat any time I'm away from my home as traveling, even if sometimes it may be overnight or for two or three days only. **Short sojourns can be as rewarding and powerful as super long trips** – they are not to be downgraded in your mind as they can be equally wonderful opportunities for each of us to be motivated to get out there.

It also means that you can refine your traveling style – discover whether you are 'a Lugger' or whether you travel lightly. You've then got time to work out any kinks, such as being under-prepared for walking long distances to 'see the

sights' or not having the right gear or simply being out of your comfort zone and away from the familiar. Redress these things when you get back and before you embark on longer trips away. Bigger isn't necessarily better when it comes to traveling. I think it's sometimes even better just to be able to go somewhere for a week, or even two weeks, knowing that you won't be gone indefinitely. You can still come home to your life without having to pack it up entirely.

One pay-off of short trips is that you get to have the excitement of going away but saving up for it doesn't take forever. A lot can happen in a short time. I'm a big fan of the short trip – lots of them in fact! You can jam a short trip chock-a-block full of activities, knowing you'll be home again shortly to recover from all the fun and games back in your own bed!

" CERTAINLY, **TRAVEL** IS MORE THAN THE SEEING OF SIGHTS; IT IS THE **CHANGE** THAT GOES ON, **DEEP** AND **PERMANENT,** IN THE IDEAS OF LIVING. "

MIRIAM BEARD
AUTHOR

TOURIST VERSUS TRAVELER

The oldest argument in the world of travel centers around who is a 'Tourist', as opposed to who is a 'Traveler'. This apparently has to do with the completely un-provable notion of who does the 'real' traveling. (Hint: supposedly the 'Traveler' does the 'real' traveling.) Here's my ten cents, for what it's worth:

In my travels **I have seen so-called tourists be travelers and so-called travelers be tourists**. The point is not what you call yourself – whoever visits a country where they are not a citizen is a 'blow-in' to the people who live there – the **difference to me lies solely in how you treat the local people**, and indeed anyone whom you meet as you go, while you are in the act of traveling.

There's a strong argument that tourism, whether package or otherwise, helps provide jobs – especially in developing countries – and is helpful and even essential in assisting communities to grow. To me, anyone who bargains too aggressively with locals for goods and services that are priced vastly below what they are used to paying at home, or who doesn't pay or tip properly, and/or who doesn't give back in any tangible way to the communities that they 'travel' through, is the same as any other person who lacks a certain sensitivity.

49

How you travel is a direct reflection of who you are as a person and no definition can make you better or worse. Whether you are away for two weeks, two months or two years, the upshot is that what counts is how 'conscious' you are while you are away.

IF TRAVELING TEACHES US ANYTHING, IT IS NEVER TO ASSUME ANYTHING.

It also teaches us – or reminds us – to have compassion. How much money you have or how much your trip costs has no bearing on your qualities as a person, let alone as one who is a guest in another country. I have seen older couples in their retirement years traveling on a packaged group tour take the time out to have proper, interested conversations with the waiters, taxi drivers and vendors they encounter on their travels. I have seen groovy backpackers wearing iPods and expensive sunglasses pretend not to see the railway station

baggage handlers who rely on the small tips to feed their families or be indifferent to wait staff who are trying their best. I have seen the parents of families who are traveling first-class instructing their children to give their personal toys to the local homeless street children. I have seen people of almost every persuasion, gender and nationality behaving well and badly – both at home and abroad. **Basically I have seen every cliché and well-worn theory about traveling proved and then disproved**.

If tourism in whatever format helps people to learn about and experience other cultures and ways of being, then it is the key to generating tolerance. Labels don't matter. They are simply another form of intolerance.

SO DON'T BE A TRAVEL SNOB!
INSPIRED TRAVELING HAS NOTHING TO DO WITH STEREOTYPES AND EVERYTHING TO DO WITH A HIGHER EXPERIENCE.

WHERE TO START. WELL, I'M A 22 YEAR OLD CHICK WHO LIVES IN THE SUNNY STATE OF QUEENSLAND. IN SEPTEMBER I AM OFF TO START MY FIRST SOLO ADVENTURE IN NEW ZEALAND.

TRAVEL HAS ALWAYS BEEN A HIGH PRIORITY TO ME. SOMETHING I HAVE ALWAYS WANTED TO DO BEFORE SETTLING DOWN. I THINK TRAVEL BROADENS YOUR HORIZONS AND MAKES YOU MORE APPRECIATIVE OF WHAT YOU REALLY DO HAVE.

A QUOTE I LOVE WHEN IT COMES TO TRAVEL IS: "WE WANDER FOR DISTRACTION, BUT WE TRAVEL FOR FULFILLMENT."

I ENCOURAGE ALL YOU GIRLS OUT THERE TO REMEMBER THIS: FIND YOURSELF, FIND YOUR GOALS, AND FIND WHAT MAKES YOU HAPPY. ENJOY YOUR OWN COMPANY AND APPRECIATE YOURSELVES. AND, TRAVEL!!!

BELINDA HENDERSON
GIRLOSOPHER

CHAPTER 2
PLANNING

WHEN I TRAVEL, I NATURALLY MEET MANY OTHER GIRLS WHO ARE TRAVELING TOO. OFTEN, THEY ARE ON THEIR OWN AND HAVE NO 'REAL' PLANS FOR THE FUTURE.

They all say, 'I'm going here next and then after that, who knows?' Their plans are at the whim of their hearts, and they allow desire and inspiration to guide them to their next destination. Living your life like this is not so easy. The expectations for most of us involve some combination of getting and keeping a 9 to 5 job and having a mortgage, or even a partner, husband and/or child in tow. Living outside the grid, as I call it, is hard to do with societal norms heavy on our shoulders. Friends and family say, 'isn't it time you settled down?' I love traveling and meeting other women who have said 'no!' to convention and, instead, find peace and satisfaction in their travels and the people they meet outside the grid.

Me?

I'm on the 'No Plan' plan!

LIZZIE NUNN
GIRLOSOPHER AND OWNER
ESCAPE SURF SAFARIS FOR WOMEN

PAUSE AND EFFECT

Travel allows us to slow things down even though at the same time we rev things up! The momentum of daily life can seem relentless from time to time, and with that comes a somewhat dimming of the senses. When that happens, the day-to-day can begin to seem tedious, and we lose that 'shine'.

HAVING A TRAVEL PLAN TO LOOK FORWARD TO PUTS A GLOSS ON EVEN THE GRAYEST OF DAYS.

While you may be having just a long weekend away that takes advantage of cheap flights, or three days camping in a nearby national park, the anticipated pleasure of being away is often lure enough to put a smile on your dial in the weeks leading up to it, and your time away can feel longer than it is. Travel plans allow you to really squeeze more zest out of the time that you have. **There's nothing like newness to make you appreciate the time you have!** That's why a last-minute trip away can be as thrilling as the one you spent ages prepping for.

No matter what sort of plan you devise for yourself, making a travel plan is liberating because if nothing else it hits the 'PAUSE' button so clearly. **Claim back time by breaking routines and going with the flow**. This alone can be a life lesson in active surrendering – something we should do as often and as thoughtfully as we can.

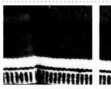

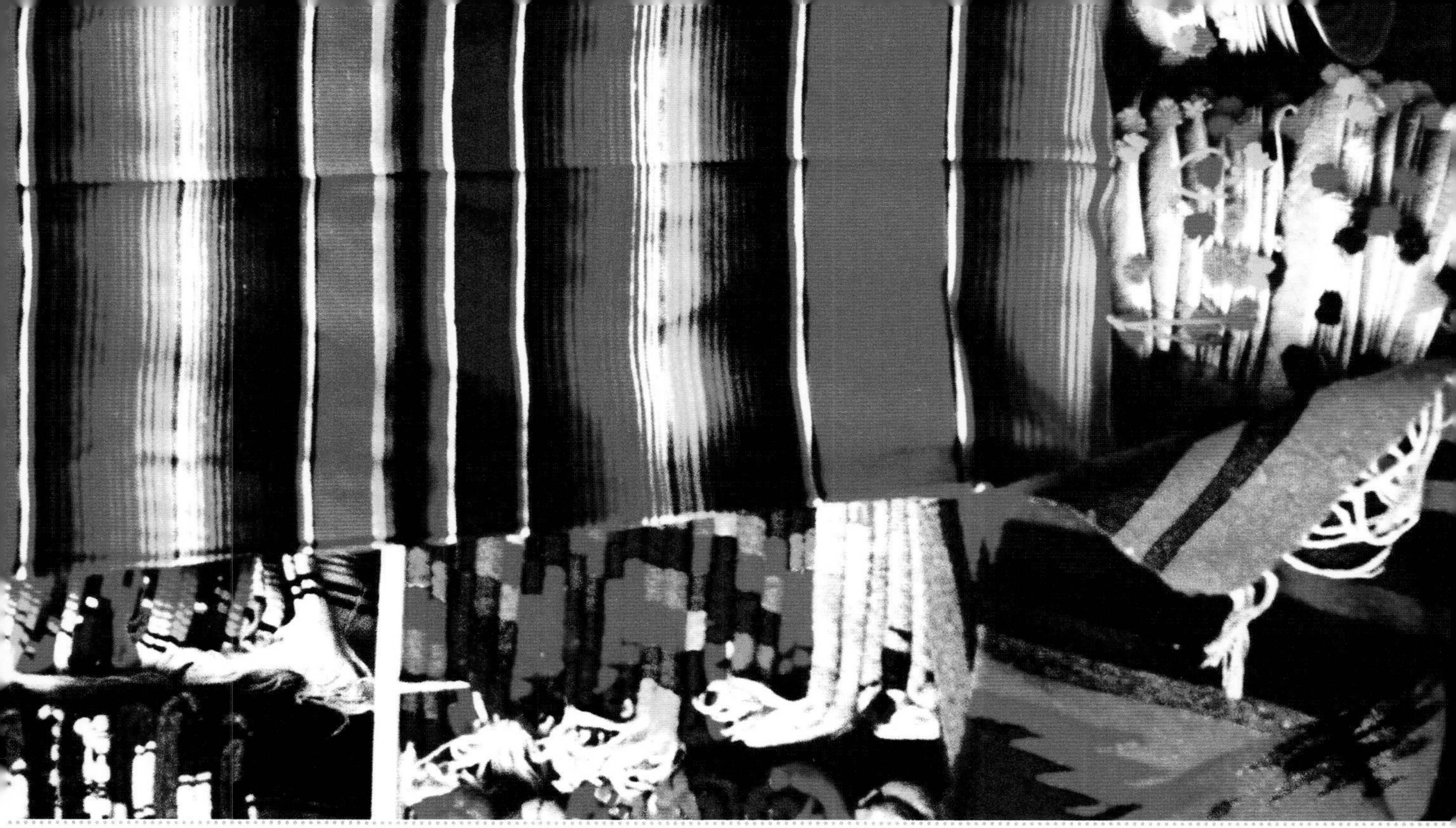

KNOWING THE RULES

You can choose to take the more casual and confident approach to travel, as does girlosopher Lizzie Nunn who calls her approach to life as living outside the 'grid', adding cheerfully, 'I'm on the "No Plan" plan!' But to have a 'No Plan' approach you kinda need to be a pretty experienced traveler like Lizzie, or one with a lot of support. In the early stages, though, I firmly believe a plan is helpful if not essential. **You can always disregard your plans later, when you're already on your way, or change them or 'suspend' them for a time it suits you and it feels right for you.**

As I have said before, even though there are exceptions to everything, for most of us a rough idea about what we intend to do and where we intend to go helps us to visualize what we might need to do in order to make it happen. But then again with the 'No Plan' plan – and here's one of the weird and somewhat unknowable contradictions of traveling –

YOU REALLY HAVE TO KNOW THE RULES BEFORE YOU CAN BEND THE RULES (OR BREAK THEM!).

PLANNING FOR DESTINY

Now that you have some idea about where you want to travel to, the next logical step is to create a plan for how to make it happen. There is a lot to do between visualizing leaving home for far-flung places and actually doing it! **A plan gives you a starting point to ensure you cover all your bases**.

Anyone who aspires to be a traveler needs some kind of a plan, if only because it becomes the yardstick by which to measure progress. Your plans show you clearly how close – or far off – your dream (and therefore your dream destination) really is. **A plan opens the doors**.

A plan always holds the glorious upside of potential. A plan highlights the opportunity we each have to change destiny by making new decisions, bringing in fresh ideas and releasing long-held fears or old patterns. A plan is the supreme tool in your arsenal of creative life skills. **Once you have a plan to go somewhere or to do something in a new place, you have found the key to creating a new future for yourself**.

It is often said that the definition of insanity is doing the same thing over and over again and expecting a different result.

TRAVELING PUTS ALL PRECONCEIVED OUTCOMES INTO THE WINDS OF DESTINY.

MAKE TRAVEL PLANS PART OF YOUR LIFE PLAN

We all have school, study, part-time or full-time work and family obligations, sometimes a combination of these commitments, and as a result our lives can seem almost completely mapped-out, with precious little breaks in the proceedings. On reflection you may come to realize that like all of us, you are – or your life is – fairly 'planned' already. The question you have is: '**How can I find time to plan to travel, let alone travel?**'

There are many ways to create the mental space and therefore real space and time to allow travel to organically become part of your life and your life plan. These strategies might not look or sound like much – it could simply be a general thought such as: 'I'll work for another four months, save up more money and then take the next six months off and travel through South America, before going back to university and finishing my course' – but that's a plan. It may seem daunting initially but sometimes all you need is an incentive to work hard, a goal to bring you to a new turning point.

TRAVEL, LIKE MOST THINGS IN LIFE, IS BEST SERVED WITH FULL INTENTION.

And just as the weavers of the best rugs in Turkey obviously know from hard experience, you can take it bit by bit, but be sure to pay careful attention to detail as you go. **Weave your dreams into your daily reality** and you can truly create something special in – and for – your life.

COMMIT AND
BE COMMITTED

No matter if you feel you lack a 'Big Picture'
view for your current or future life, you'll
find there is actually always a hazy plan of
some sort hovering around you. It is hard for
most of us to think ahead in five- or ten-year
periods, however, the old saying, **'If you don't
know where you're going, then how will you
know when you get there?'**, also makes a bit of
sense. You need at least a vague idea of what
you'd like to be doing so that you can build
some solid foundations for it to happen. Maybe
you can only think about a month away to begin
with. But once you get used to being in travel
mode, you should be able to plan for longer
periods of time.

**To start with, it might be easier to work out a
plan for one year**. And if you still think that's
too hard, then break the year down into months.
What is on your agenda this month? Next month?
What are you doing later in the summer? What
immediate and ongoing commitments do you have?
We all have some – and here's a secret – even
commitment-phobics have commitments!

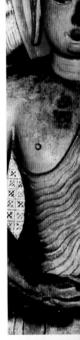

Grab a calendar or your diary and check out on
paper how many days of the week or month you do
activities. Make a list of all of the things you
are involved in (whether it is school, friends,
sports events, university, your family, a
relationship, work, flatmates, pets, projects,
hobbies or charities you regularly contribute
to) and you will soon be able to sketch out how
these impact on your time on a month-to-month
basis.

Where is your free time, committed time and (importantly) your down time allocated? Do any of your projects or commitments have a natural or built-in conclusion that will allow you to vary things? The end of school is a classic –

WHY NOT MAKE USE OF THE ENDLESS SUMMER TO SHRUG ON A BACKPACK AND GO EXPLORING?

It's a much better use of your time than waiting for that boy to call you back!

Once you have made the list, you can then fill out what the rest of the year looks like. And from this new bird's-eye look at all the nano-details of your world you might just see where some travel can be fitted into your scheme of things.

COLORING IN
YOUR BIG PICTURE

Your plan will, more than likely, alert you to what you may need to put on hold (job, relationship, university course, family expectations) and what sacrifices you may have to make (not taking a promotion or earning less money, being single, late graduation, being away for important family events) in order to fulfill your dreams of travel. **Try not to focus on what you may miss out on; rather, put energy into the positive things that could come as a result of your plans** (a better job because of your experiences and therefore more income, a new relationship, a change in your studies that is better for you long-term, your family coming to visit you while you are in another country, giving you a whole new perspective on your relationships).

THE PLAN HELPS FORM THE PICTURE SO YOU CAN COLOR IN THE LINES.

You need an idea of how long you'd like to travel for, because that will then tell you the kinds of bigger, more life-impacting decisions that you will need to make.

SRI VIS

THE FORCE
IS WITH YOU!

Once you have worked out your immediate life plan, and earmarked the time you can set aside for a trip, there is the next stage of planning. It comes with commitment (there's that word again). When you actually commit to something, you set in motion the universal forces that will assist you to realize the plan.

It's amazing how quickly these things can get going. For example, you decide to go to Canada to learn French and

begin making inquiries, researching online and building up your savings account. All of a sudden your mother mentions a friend of hers has relatives in Montreal whom you might be able to stay with. They happen to have friends with a ski lodge at Mount Whistler and children about your age. Before you know it, you are in North America, snowboarding with a cute boy who has a ton of friends, so your social **life while you are away has just fallen into place**.

AS A RESULT OF EVEN A VAGUE PLAN, YOU WILL OFTEN BE AMAZED TO FIND THAT YOUR WORLD IS SUDDENLY MUCH, MUCH LARGER. BELIEVE ME, IT HAPPENS ALL THE TIME!

"I HAVE BEEN THINKING ABOUT YOUR WISE WORDS ON THE PHONE WHEN I ANNOUNCED THAT I WILL HAVE TO POSTPONE MY TRAVELS: 'LET'S SEE WHAT WILL BE IN MARCH.'

IN FACT, I WON'T BE MAKING IT
THIS MARCH,
BUT HAVE PLANNED THE TRIP
FOR SEPTEMBER.
[SO] THE PLAN IS STILL THE SAME,
JUST THE TIMING A BIT LATER.
BEFORE I MAKE
A DECISION ON A POTENTIAL
MOVE,
I NEED TO
SEE SOME THINGS
THROUGH HERE.

THERE IS A TIME
FOR EVERYTHING.
NINA NAASE
GIRLOSOPHER AND INTREPID TRAVELER
GERMANY

HOMEWORK ... AND AWAY

Obviously the more you know in advance about something the better your chances of maximizing the success of the venture. This is certainly true about traveling. Doing your homework before you make a single booking will give you a much-needed heads-up on what to expect and how to make your trip as optimal and as cost-effective as possible. **Here are a few GIRLO tips to get the lowdown on your chosen destination(s):**

- READ, READ, READ! Check out travel magazines and newsletters, as well as books, both fiction and non-fiction.
- GO ONLINE and Google Earth. Check it all out from space – in 3-D!
- Google destinations, accommodations and reviews (see the list of websites in the back section on pp 240 to 247.

- SPEAK TO A FEW TRAVEL AGENTS. Even if you don't end up booking with them you never know what they may be able to tell you; it could be information that will be invaluable for your trip planning.
- READ THE TRAVEL SECTIONS OF NEWSPAPERS, usually written by well-funded travel journalists who do the hard miles so others can follow. The articles also refer to websites of interest and are often the first to note a new place, so you can beat the hordes if you're up on it!
- READ THE CLASSIFIEDS and keep your eyes open for special flights and deals. MAKE NOTES, take interest and be well-briefed on what is on offer.
- BE AWARE THAT AIRPORT AND DEPARTURE TAXES CAN ADD UP TO 20 PERCENT in some cases to the cost of the flight. Look out for other 'hidden' surprises so you're not taken unawares when the bills come in.

If success in anything is the result of opportunity meeting preparation, there's no doubt this is doubly so when it comes to traveling. The idea is to get as much info under your belt before you go away, to maximize your chances of having a great travel experience and getting the most out of your time away. Whatever you choose to do before you leave may seem totally different in how it impacts on you once you're away and things are set in motion plan-wise. **Contacts, accommodation, transport, guides, activities, travel requirements are all best thought out in advance with as much fact-checking as possible.** And the more general knowledge you have about your destination, the more you will have a sense of things, and the better you'll respond if things are not going to plan (read: pear-shaped!). Information is power and it helps you to do the important things while you are away – like relaxing for example!

Good old guidebook(s) are a mainstay – doubly useful when you're away and you face those inevitable delayed flight or flat-tire moments; **you can read up on your next port of call!** Now guide books are more demographically targeted and regularly updated, so of course these are an excellent source of information. They all have great online resources too.

OPPORTUNITY + PREPARATION = SUCCESS

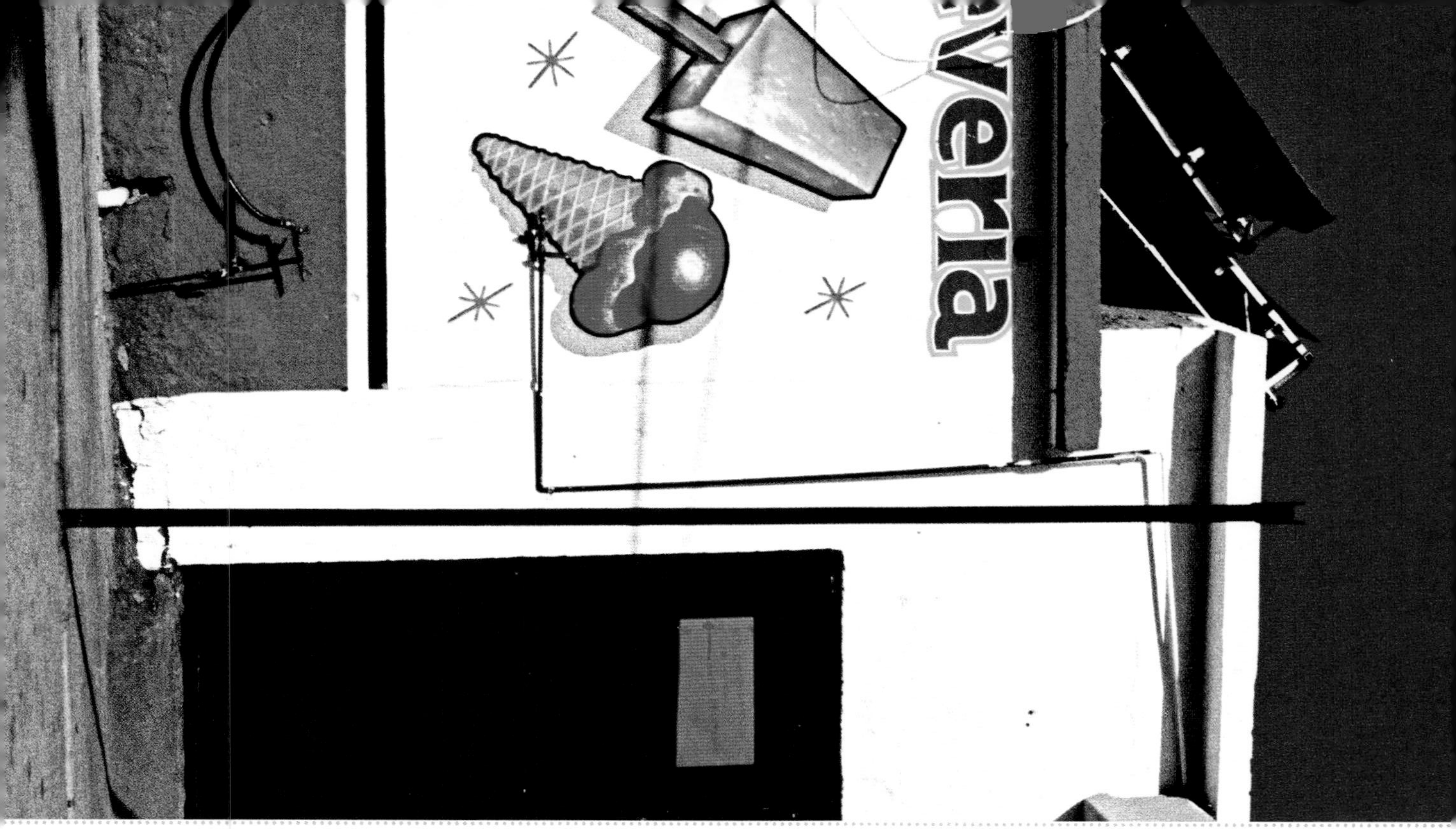
veria

DOLLARS AND SENSE

Well we all know the hard truth: you need money when you travel. So a budget is a critical part of any travel plan. Whether you want to go away for three days or three years, you absolutely need to work out the money side carefully – as soon as you can – so you don't run into financial troubles thousands of miles away from home.

YOU SHOULD TREAT BOTH YOUR RESEARCH AND YOUR BUDGET LIKE YOU WOULD ANY PROJECT.

Try to budget a daily rate for your travels. Let's say you have a 21-day trip trekking through Asia. You might work out that you need a maximum of so much per day for all your expenses. Multiply that amount by 21 to get a total-trip calculation. **Once you have worked out a (realistic) figure, not only can you work out a plan to save this amount, you can plan for a little bit on top to go towards some shopping or extra fun activities, etc**.

Along the way you may find ways to save a bit from your budget. For instance, you may budget to share the hire of a taxi from the airport between you and your traveling companion but in the queue you meet other people needing a lift to the same place so you travel together, saving a little along the way.

HOT GIRLO MONEY TIPS

• Create a spreadsheet with all the categories of expenses you are likely to encounter so you can make sense of where your hard-earned dollars will be needed and so that you don't miss anything along the way! You can add more categories as you go if necessary.

HOT GIRLO MONEY TIPS

• Consult travel guide books and foreign exchange websites to get a sense of what your dollar will buy in the country you will be visiting (see back section). A travel agent can also be a helpful resource to ensure you get an accurate cost of flights and transfers (and they almost always know cool stuff about places!).

HOT GIRLO MONEY TIPS

• If you are doing your bookings online get someone else to double-check them before you confirm them to ensure you haven't missed anything, especially if you think you may need to change your flights at any time. There are penalties with some cheap fares and if you need to change a flight or booking you can sometimes find yourself paying the (increased) difference between the discount rate and the full fare plus a fee for making the change.

HOT GIRLO MONEY TIPS

• Ask your parents or an accountant for guidance on other hidden costs, like travel insurance, tipping, excess baggage (say for sporting equipment, etc.) and hotel or accommodation taxes.

HOT GIRLO MONEY TIPS

• Ask advice from an experienced traveler who has either been to the places you are planning to go to or who will be able to help you compile a realistic list of all of the expenses you can expect to incur on a long-term trip.

If you stay on top of your spending on a daily basis, you are less inclined to blow it on unnecessary things and that means you are even less likely to have a problem while you're away. Here are a few more things to think about for your budget:

• BEFORE THE TRIP:
Even while you are saving up (especially if it's a long-term plan) you still have to live. A budget before you leave will keep you on track financially and give you a sense of purpose and progress while you save. It will also serve to remind you about some of the sacrifices you'll have to make!

• DURING THE TRIP:
While you are on the road, unexpected costs can come in all forms. An extra ticket you hadn't planned on buying or an unexpected airline excess baggage cost can wreak havoc with your bank balance. Likewise the replacement for any lost property while you're away. Even if these can be claimed back later through insurance, you will still need to have cash available to replace lost items. So factor in a little extra for while you are away.

· AFTER THE TRIP:

It's often overlooked but having at least a small nest egg for when you get home is important. It maybe OK for a while to rely on your parents or friends when you're back but being flat broke – that gets old really quickly! It is far better to save up enough to cover you for at least 4 to 6 weeks of living expenses once you get home again. This is especially so if you don't have a job of any sort to come home to or if you are not studying (i.e. if you're a student at a tertiary level you may be eligible for a student allowance). Having even a modest amount of money to come home to will make you feel more empowered and make your re-entry a softer landing.

HOT GIRLO MONEY TIPS

Carry a debit card (the opposite of a credit card!) that holds an 'Emergency cash only' lump sum – but you must only use this in a crisis. You need a bit of discipline but you'll be grateful if you do need to access it! That way you're not using credit (which costs money if it goes into the period that incurs interest); instead you've got your own money to use when additional costs appear unexpectedly.

ON THE (PAPER) TRAIL

Imagine if you lost your bag with all your original trip itinerary, passport, traveler's checks, travel insurance forms, etc., while you were away. **We all want to save trees, but there really are some things you need to have a copy of!** A small file or envelope containing photocopies of all your travel documents should be left with your parents or Bestie. You could even keep it somewhere safe, say in your filing cabinet at home, where it will be relatively easy for someone to access while you are away. It will be a relief to know you can still pick up the phone and everything you need is right there or just a fax or email away. **Create your file as you plan your trip and add in copies of the following as you get them:**

•	PASSPORT	photocopy of all pages including clear copies of all current visas.
•	DRIVER'S LICENCE OR PHOTO ID	you should have a copy of these.
•	COMPLETE ITINERARY	with full details of all accommodation reservation reference numbers, flights, bookings, contact details and names as relevant.
•	PAYMENT SLIPS	for any pre-bookings, reservations, advance payments, travel vouchers, etc.
•	WRITTEN CORRESPONDENCE	and printouts of emails that confirm your travel arrangements, payments, etc.
•	CONTACT DETAILS	the full names, home and email addresses of all people whom you are planning on staying with (friends or contacts) or perhaps even just catching up with when you are traveling.
•	TRAVEL INSURANCE DOCUMENTS	containing clear dates of your insurance cover plus proof of payment.
•	LETTERS OF REFERRAL	if you are going to be an exchange student or working with a charity. Also, add in copies of school reports, academic certifications, other achievements or awards – these are probably relevant only if you are planning to be away for a year or more.

• AN UP-TO-DATE RESUME	just in case it needs to be sent somewhere – for a course, job, college, scholarship application, etc. – while you are away.
• LIST OF BANK ACCOUNTS	you are planning on accessing while you are away.
• LIST OF ALL DEBIT AND CREDIT CARDS	all the details of the cards you will be using while you are away. These should include the visual pin number that is usually on the reverse of the cards and the billing address for each (these are both sometimes needed to prove validity over a phone identity check). Do NOT write down your secret pin numbers for any account or card – you should never give these out.
• PHOTOCOPIES OF TRAVELER'S CHECKS	or note down all the serial numbers on a sheet of paper and keep a copy in the file.
• PHONE NUMBERS	or other contact details for people at home – just in case they're needed while you are away. These can be your flatmate's, or boyfriend's details, and include your traveling companion's details, such as their parents, family, etc., as well as details of your group leader, teacher, guide, chaperone or guardian if relevant.

Just remember, the whole point of the paper trail is to make it less stressful for both you and your family (or whoever is looking after these documents for you) to access your personal information in an emergency. It's about being considerate and **making life easier for everyone!** Just think: if you needed something urgently and didn't have this file, someone else would have to spend a lot of their time and energy to help you, and this could cause them huge problems. Although it is a bit of work to prepare, it is more about being thoughtful of others. **Ultimately, it is about being responsible.**

HOT GIRLO TIP

Scan all the documents listed above and email them to your own personal travel email address, another good way to access the information in an emergency. Don't just rely on this, however, as you may find yourself in a place where they don't have internet access.

HOT GIRLO TIP

Always keep spare passport-sized photographs with you and in the file. These are incredibly helpful to have if you ever need to replace your passport or lodge any urgent visa applications.

HOT GIRLO TIP

Traveler's checks are kind of an old-fashioned way to carry currency when you are away, but the beauty of them is that if you are in a remote area that doesn't have ATM access or credit or debit cards, they are ready cash – provided of course that you can show a photo ID. They are relatively secure and can also be replaced pretty quickly if you lose them or if they are stolen. It beats carrying around a lot of the local currency, which can be a magnet for thieves.

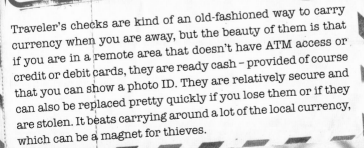

COUNTING DOWN TO LIFT-OFF

Once you have a sense of how, when and where you are going, Once you have a sense of how, when and where you are going, you then need to figure out the timeframes and what you have to do prior to leaving. Don't leave tasks to the last week – in the flurry of farewell parties, packing, parting with all your friends and family, you'll have enough on your plate!

Create a timeline counting down the days till you leave. You'll be surprised how quickly 187 days turns into 2! Not only will it serve to keep you on track with your savings plan, it will keep you motivated to check off those lists of things to do.

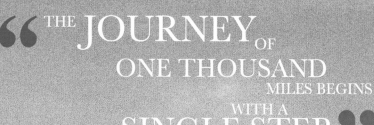
" THE JOURNEY OF
ONE THOUSAND
MILES BEGINS
WITH A

SINGLE STEP. "
LAO TZU

LAO TZU QUOTE

87

PLANNING

CHAPTER 3
PREPARATION

statue of 'Pushkin', an admired
very famous Russian Poet.
e was killed in a duel with
Frenchman over his wife, and
hat is how he died. There are
any statues throughout Moscow
nd also coloured Xmas Trees
er the Xmas Period. Xmas is
ent on the 7th of Jan, using
e Julian calendar, Russians
e either Orthodox or
atholic, mainly orthodox.
e weather was dull most of the
me we were there. Smoggy +
old! "The Sun takes of Russian
History"

> IN 2005, I DID A FUNDRAISING GIG TO RAISE
> MONEY TO SAVE THE WILD BACTRIAN
> CAMEL FROM BECOMING EXTINCT IN
> CHINA. WE RAISED ENOUGH MONEY TO
> HELP FEED TWO BABY BACTRIAN CAMELS
> AND WHEN I WENT TO THE UK I VISITED
> THE FOUNDER OF THE WILD CAMEL
> PROTECTION FOUNDATION (WCPF) WHO
> WE DONATED THE MONEY TO. WE HAD
> A LOVELY TIME TALKING CAMELS AND
> TRADING ADVENTURE STORIES.

It's a small world.

ROMY CAMPBELL HICKS
GIRLOSOPHER AND CONSERVATIONIST

ROMY CAMPBELL HICKS
GIRLOSOPHER AND CONSERVATIONIST

PAGE # 89

CHAPTER # 3

CHAPTER
PREPARATION

BELIEVE AND IT SHALL BE

If you have in your mind that you will be a successful traveler, then that will be your experience. While it is a complete projection into the future (especially when you're sitting on the couch at home!), your thoughts around the whole venture will determine how you approach the trip and, consequently, how you go once you're on the road. When you feel in control from the outset and things then don't go according to plan, you'll be in a much better position to go with the new flow. You'll emerge unruffled more often than not.

Prepare to be successful and envisage a life-changing trip where you are ready but flexible; where you are open to the experience yet capable of managing any situation. Once you have made your timeline and you are counting down the days until you are taxiing down the runway, the most important thing to do is to get into serious preparation mode.

If you are not necessarily an experienced traveler, you'll need to get in some practice before you leave the comfort of your sofa. That way if you find things difficult, you can recover in the comfort of home while you regroup. In this section we'll plan to get you into efficient packing mode and even **run through the steps of a 'small' trip away to give you a taste of the wonderful adventure to come before the big trip**.

VISAS - YOUR TICKET IN

It's essential to possess the correct 'tourist' visa or 'working' visa for the country you wish to travel or work in. Not having a visa means you have either entered with a visa which has since expired (called 'overstaying your visa') or you do not possess the correct one for the purposes of your travels (you may have entered on a tourist visa but you are working and do not possess a working visa).

Without a visa you would be traveling or working illegally and there is no protection for you as a worker, nor from the immigration authorities who are increasingly taking more aggressive approaches to policing this. You could end up being deported - for which they do not need to give you any notice - it can be as sudden as the same day or within 24 hours. This may result in a temporary or lifetime ban from entering the country again.

SO DO YOUR HOMEWORK AND GET THE RIGHT VISA!

BAGGAGE ... WHAT ARE YOU TAKING?

It's a cliché, but it's true: **your bag is your portable home while you are away**. Making sure you have the correct one (or combination of bags) for your needs before you go ensures a smooth travel-style. Choosing your bag(s) is crucial.
Look for:

- STRONG HANDLES AND STRAPS
- EASY ACCESS MULTI-ZIPPERED COMPARTMENTS
- ROOMY INTERIOR WITH LAYERS
- GOOD SECURITY FEATURES, SUCH AS ZIPS THAT 'LOCK IN'
- LIGHT WEIGHT
- WATER RESISTANT, IF POSSIBLE.

If your trip is going to be a mixture of town 'n' country you should **go for a bag that is light, durable, water resistant and multipurpose**. Warning: picking a bag is a bit like working out what shoes to wear with an outfit – you need the right bag to go with the right trip!

THE BACKPACK

IF YOUR TRIP IS TREKKING-STYLE OR ONE INVOLVING RIDING ANIMALS OR CAMPING, YOU WILL NEED THE CORRECT BACKPACK OR SOFT BAG. IF YOU ARE GOING WITH A GROUP, CHECK WITH THE TOUR GUIDE OR ORGANIZATION AS TO THE SIZE AND FRAME-TYPE OR SPECIFIC BRAND, IF ANY, THAT THEY RECOMMEND. NORMAL SUITCASES ARE DIFFICULT IN THESE SITUATIONS DUE TO THEIR SHAPE.

THINK OF THE POOR SHERPAS!

DAY-PACK

MANY BACKPACKS HAVE A ZIP-OFF MINI PACK OR 'DAY-PACK' WHICH IS GREAT TO TAKE ON BOARD AS CABIN LUGGAGE. ZIP IT BACK ON ONCE YOU ARRIVE AT YOUR DESTINATION OR GET TO THE POINT OF TREK DEPARTURE AND YOU CAN THEN BE HANDS-FREE.

HOT GIRLO TIP

You will need lots of small padlocks to fully secure a backpack.

HANDBAG

DEPENDING ON WHO YOU ARE AND WHERE YOU'RE GOING, A HANDBAG CAN STILL WORK FOR THE PLANE OR WHEN SIGHTSEEING AROUND URBAN CENTERS. IF IT'S NEW YORK, LONDON, PARIS, MILAN OR HONG KONG, YOU'LL BE PERFECTLY PREPARED TO SWAN THROUGH THE LOBBY OF ANY HOTEL WITH A CHIC CARRY-ALL ON YOUR ARM. ON THE OTHER HAND, IF YOU'RE PART OF A GROUP TREKKING THE HIMALAYAS, YOUR GUIDE WILL QUITE POSSIBLY FALL OFF THE SIDE OF THE MOUNTAIN IN NEPAL IF YOU EMERGE FROM YOUR HUT WITH THE LATEST FASHION SHOULDER BAG. YOU HAVE BEEN WARNED!

CAMERA BAG

IF YOU WANT TO LOOK LIKE A PRO WHEN YOU'RE TRAVELING, TAKE A PADDED CAMERA BAG AND IT CAN DOUBLE AS YOUR HAND LUGGAGE. THEY ARE USUALLY REALLY WELL-DESIGNED AND HAVE TONS OF COOL COMPARTMENTS TO STASH ALL YOUR BITS 'N' PIECES FOR THE FLIGHT. NOT TO MENTION THEY KEEP YOUR CAMERA AND ACCESSORIES SAFE AND SNUG. THEY COME WITH NORMAL HANDLES, SINGLE SHOULDER STRAP OR YOU CAN GET THE BACKPACK VERSIONS, WHICH ARE ALSO PADDED.

HOSTIE BAG

IF YOU ARE GOING 'URBAN', AND TRIPS BETWEEN, SAY, AIRPORTS AND HOTELS MEAN LONG WALKS, A GREAT OPTION IS A SMALL OVERNIGHT BAG ON WHEELS THAT YOU CAN CARRY ON BOARD THE PLANE. THESE COME WITH ZIPPERED COMPARTMENTS AND A LONG RETRACTABLE HANDLE SO YOU CAN STACK OTHER BITS AND PIECES ON TOP – ALL THE FLIGHT ATTENDANTS USE THESE. AGAIN, PADLOCKS ARE ESSENTIAL FOR THIS BAG.

MAIN BAG

WHAT YOU NEED HERE IS WHEELS, BABY. IF YOU DO CHOOSE A NORMAL SUITCASE, CHOOSE ONE THAT ALSO HAS BOTH WHEELS AND A FULLY RETRACTABLE LONG HANDLE. GO FOR A FIRM EXTERIOR IF YOU ARE CHOOSING A TRADITIONAL CASE.

IF YOU PREFER A SOFTER OR MORE UTILITARIAN-STYLE BAG, THE SURFING/CAMPING/SAILING-STYLE BAGS OFTEN HAVE WHEELS AND THEY ARE IDEAL IF YOU'RE NOT CARRYING BREAKABLES. BY THE WAY, YOU SHOULD TRY NOT TO PACK BREAKABLES. IT'S TOO RISKY AND I CAN TELL YOU FROM PERSONAL EXPERIENCE THAT LUGGING SOMETHING HALFWAY AROUND THE WORLD ONLY TO HAVE CUSTOMS TELL YOU IT'S GOING THROUGH THE BAGGAGE X-RAY IN A MILLION PIECES IS ... DISAPPOINTING, TO SAY THE LEAST.

BAGS THAT ARE COLORED TEND TO SHOW THE DIRT AND – IN MY OPINION – ATTRACT ATTENTION. BLACK IS COOL AND UNDER THE RADAR. USE BRIGHT TAGS, A COLORED LUGGAGE STRAP THAT GOES AROUND THE OUTSIDE OF THE WHOLE BAG, OR A SMALL RIBBON ON THE STRAP TO EASILY IDENTIFY YOUR BAG AS IT COMES OFF THE BAGGAGE CAROUSEL.

THE MAIN THING TO KEEP IN MIND WITH YOUR MAIN BAG IS THE WEIGHT – A SUITCASE SHOULD FEEL SUPER LIGHT WHEN IT'S EMPTY.

THE BIG LUGGAGE SECRET

Well many years of travel has taught me that **no matter what you think you won't buy while you are away, you will always buy more stuff than you should**. So pack **a small water-resistant canvas 'camping style' soft bag that can be folded flat** and store it in the outside zippered compartment of your main bag. Yes, it's kind of 'cheating' a bit, and you may have to pay a small amount for overweight luggage on the flight home, but at least you'll be able to get the cushion covers that you bought in that bazaar in Morocco home ... of course they are a present for Nanna!

PSST! WHAT'S IN THE BAG?

The idea is not to have a groaningly heavy bag that you can't manage by yourself. If you have that much stuff, it is far better to spread the weight across a couple of bags that you can at least lift and stack on a trolley if you find yourself on your own and without a porter in sight. And it is a certainty that you will.

If you are traveling with a friend then you can both fill the smaller spare bag with the heavy stuff and split any overweight luggage costs between you.

HOT GIRLO TIP

When it comes to baggage, cheap is not always cheerful! You'll pay for it many times over at the weigh-in later if the frame is a heavy one. Go for a light frame, which sometimes means paying a bit more for the bag in the first place. Think of it this way, buy it well, buy it once. You'll be grateful when it's fully packed!

> WHEN PREPARING TO TRAVEL, LAY OUT ALL YOUR CLOTHES AND ALL YOUR MONEY. THEN TAKE HALF THE CLOTHES AND TWICE THE MONEY.

HOT GIRLO TIPPING STRATEGY

Where possible get baggage handlers to assist you. Trust me, whatever it costs, it's always worth the tip! Which – by the way – you really should be prepared to do and be prepared for at all times. I keep small notes of the local currency tucked into a jeans' pocket or jacket's button down pocket so I can tip quickly without struggling to open my purse or wallet, etc. A stack of one-dollar notes is always appreciated by porters so they don't have to change a large bill in the local – usually black – currency market and they won't get queried or run into problems as a result. Tip them at the very end of the service.

HOW AND WHAT TO PACK WHERE

How to pack is a discussion that is as old as traveling, such as, should you roll your clothes or pack them flat? Well actually, both! Some items cry out to be rolled, others never recover from it! Trial and error I find is the only thing that works here. But the general rule is that natural fibers tend to crease more and synthetic blends will be better rolled (but often can't be ironed). Roll singlets, sweaters, polo-necks, hoodies, tracksuits, pajamas and jeans. Pack flat and use dry cleaning bags on anything light such as cotton shirts or dresses. Use those mesh washing bags or large format zip-lock plastic bags to separate and bundle bras, undies, socks and swimwear. A bonus is that separating things makes them easier to find. Bagging them in plastic protects them from water and/or unintended damp clothes from washing, too.

TECHNIQUES FOR LIFTING
Bend your knees, place both hands firmly around the handles and keeping a straight back, lifting in a single fluid upwards motion until you are standing upright. Let go of one hand if that feels more comfortable. Careful lifting will mean that you don't spend your entire holiday at the doctors or on the massage table trying to recover from the effort!

DAY PACK/HANDBAG /IN-CABIN LUGGAGE

SMALL FOLD-UP UMBRELLA:
Keep this in the side pocket for easy access. Great for the unexpected monsoon!

MINI TORCH:
Rechargeable if possible. At night keep this close, on the bedside table perhaps - great for power outages or to find your bag on night-time bus/train rides, or even for reading if you want to be especially considerate of the person sleeping in the seat next to you. Take spare batteries.

BLACKOUT EYE SHADES:
Never leave home without 'em. The essential traveler's friend. The silk ones feel more comfortable than the ones they give you on the plane. Buy the adjustable ones with a thick loose elastic strap as they stay on better if you have long, or super shiny hair.

BLOW-UP NECK PILLOW OR PAD:
Just as essential as the eye shades. The faux suede ones are good, but it is best not to blow them up too hard: 'squishy' works best!

GOOD SUNGLASSES:
I always travel with two pairs in separate hard cases. If you're in an urban center, losing your sunnies is annoying but not a disaster. However if you're out in the sticks on an adventure and you lose a pair, it's a dead cert there will be no Polaroid sunglasses within 50 miles!

PASHMINA:
A chic accessory at any time of the day or night and indispensable on the planes for those 'over-chilled' flights (read: old planes that are about the same cabin temperature as the air outside at 40,000 feet). You can wear it twisted around your neck or shoulders if you don't want to carry it in your pack.

CARDIGAN OR LIGHT SWEATER:
Great for layering especially once night falls. In the desert, the nights can get to freezing cold temperatures, even if it gets incredibly hot during the days. Be prepared and have another layer to hand.

HOLD-ALL FOR PASSPORT, TICKETS, ITINERARY, VOUCHERS, ETC.:
Get in the habit of always putting your passport, tickets, boarding passes, itinerary and so on back into your hold-all and get into the habit of putting it back into the same compartment of your day-pack or hand luggage. Whatever you do, don't stick your passport and other documents in the back pocket of your jeans where they can be stolen or fall out.

SMALL MINI-COSMETIC BAG OR CLEAR ZIP-LOCK BAG:
Great for lip balm, facial moisturizer, eye drops, fragrance, toothbrush, toothpaste, tissues, personal care items and a small hairbrush or comb (see security notes below).

ANTISEPTIC HANDY WIPES:
For use after dirty trolleys, finger printing at customs (in the US) and shaking a million hands upon arrival!

RESCUE REMEDY DROPS:
Available from the health food store or local pharmacy. Use a few drops on your tongue if you feel overwhelmed, emotional or stressed. Be sure to replace the lid properly after use. Seal in a small clear zip-lock plastic bag.

VITAMINS:
As you will be stressing your immune system with all that physical activity and general excitement, take supplements on board in your clear zip-lock bag, containing enough for the flight – pack the actual bottles with the major supply in your main bag. Minimum needs: vitamins B + C + Zinc + Echinacea. Take them during the flight or train ride, etc., with your meals. Remember to check with your doctor about which supplements are right for you.

SMALL BOTTLE FOR WATER:
I refill mine daily (only with bottled water though!) and I always keep it with me. Indispensable for those times when you sit delayed on runways for hours without refreshments.

NOTEBOOK/TRAVEL JOURNAL AND PEN:
You have to start writing from the very beginning of the trip. Memory can get fuzzy when you travel and things are always changing. Take note!

BOOK TO READ:
Something to keep you going while waiting on platforms, in departure lounges or during delays. Here's a good chance to learn more about your destination with a guide book or slip into another world with a fat page turner.

IPOD + CHARGER:
No explanation necessary! Invaluable to have some heavy metal to get you through the hard sections, not to mention Jamiroquai for the sunrise ... or Bob St Clair for long nights on the train or plane. It is truly a 21st century travel essential.

DIGITAL CAMERA + CHARGER:
Include a couple of extra chips if you are going to be a long way from any places where you can download your images.

POWERPOINT ADAPTOR:
For the first country you arrive in, others can go in your main bag.

TRAVELING WELL AND HAPPILY IS ABOUT
DEVELOPING GOOD HABITS THAT ALLOW YOU TO BE FREED
MENTALLY FROM WHATEVER 'BAGGAGE' YOU MAY HAVE WITH YOU.

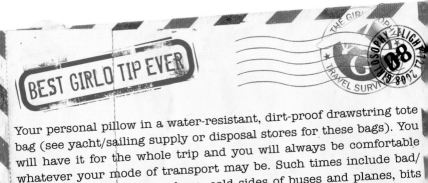

BEST GIRLO TIP EVER

Your personal pillow in a water-resistant, dirt-proof drawstring tote bag (see yacht/sailing supply or disposal stores for these bags). You will have it for the whole trip and you will always be comfortable whatever your mode of transport may be. Such times include bad/uncomfortable seats anywhere, cold sides of buses and planes, bits that stick out in the back of 4WDs, waiting on train stations for trains that threaten never to come, for taxi/mini van transfers during long, crowded peak-hour journeys to airports and crowded campervans.

THERE IS NOTHING LIKE YOUR OWN PILLOW
FOR A GOOD NIGHT'S SLEEP ANY TIME, ANYWHERE.

P.S. Use a colored – not white – pillow slip!

MAIN BAG/BACKPACK/SUITCASE

Less is more, especially when it comes to packing clothes. Your medical kit is far more important! Obviously your packing also depends on the type of trip you are making: long or short, backpacking or more urban center, beach or winter resort. Each will require a different packing list. The trick is to think about what you will wear on the plane, and every day and night while you're there, then list them. Here's a basic list for a general trans-seasonal trip of what to take from the ground up.

HOT GIRLO TIP

Mix and match all your clothing and shoes around these colors: black, white, blue denim, khaki green and a touch of red. Everything is then able to be worn together and you need less stuff – not to mention you'll always look pulled-together which is often a challenge when you're traveling.

SHOES: 1 PAIR EACH OF THESE:

RUBBER THONGS/FLIP-FLOPS/SLIPPERS:
For wearing to/at the beach and in the shower (crucial if you are staying in accommodation where the hygiene factor is less than 3 stars!).

TRAINERS:
For traveling, jogging, walking, sightseeing (great for rainy days).

SANDALS:
Flat, black, brown or neutral color (go with everything night and day).

TREKKING BOOTS:
If you are trekking or walking in wilderness. Break these in really thoroughly before you go! Nothing and no one can help you if your feet are sore and covered in blisters.

BOOTS:
Long, flat, black or dark brown leather, can be worn under jeans or with skirts, dressed up or casual.

BALLET SLIPPERS:
Black, satin, great for evening. (What's not to like? They are elegant, light and – best of all – they pack flat.)

CLOTHING

T-SHIRTS:
Long- and short-sleeved, white and colored; mixes you can layer with singlets and other Ts underneath. That way as you get warmer when the sun gets high you can de-layer and simply roll them up and stuff into a pocket of your daypack. Throw them out when they become stained or holey – easily replaced cheaply en route!

TRACKSUIT BOTTOMS:
Cotton – wear as PJs with T-shirt.

HOODIES:
Cotton, long-sleeved, zip-up front. Wear with tracky bottoms or with jeans. Great for the plane.

JEANS/TROUSERS:
1 pair blue denim jeans, 1 pair trousers like khakis or corduroy trousers.

SKIRTS:
1 – black/denim/neutral and knee length.

SWEATERS:
1 – polo-necked cotton/wool/lycra blend.

CARDIGAN:
1 – V-necked or round-necked navy, black or light-colored wool.

DENIM JACKET:
Goes with absolutely everything! Wear on the plane.

DRESS:
1 – black, short-sleeved, three-quarter length.

If you are going trekking or snowboarding you will need to add:

SNOWBOARD PANTS OR OVERALLS

SKIVVIES: 2

FLEECY-LINED LONG-SLEEVED
ZIP-UP TOP:
These pull sweat
away from your body and keep
you warm/cool/comfortable.

THERMAL UNDERWEAR

GLOVES

GOGGLES

PADDED GORE-TEX PARKA

WOOLEN NECK SCARF

THICK SOCKS:
At least 2 pairs.

REPEAT AFTER ME:
I WILL ONLY TAKE THINGS THAT
ARE PRACTICAL AND THAT I WILL ACTUALLY WEAR!

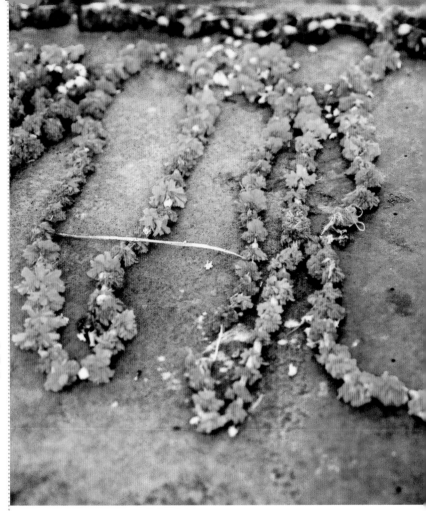

ACCESSORIES

BEANIES:
Cotton and/or woollen are best for sleeping at night in cold climates. Beanies rule!

HEAD SCARVES:
Cotton, printed for a splash of color. These hide bad hair days really well!

ONE-PIECE SWIMSUIT OR BIKINI:
Always good to have on hand – even if for a dip at the hotel's pool or for modest outdoor showering and lake baths, etc.

WHITE COTTON SOCKS:
Wear socks or you'll end up throwing out smelly sneakers.

EACH TOWEL:

othing screams 'tourist' more
han turning up on the beach with
hotel bath towel. In addition
ome backpacker places charge a
eposit and/or for the use of
wels, so if you have your own
u'll avoid it.

WATERPROOF WATCH:

Time-keeping without humidity,
surf or snow issues!

SWISS ARMY POCKETKNIFE:

Handy for peeling fruit or opening
drink bottles, fixing screws on
luggage and cutting off tags,
etc.

OTHER MISCELLANEOUS ITEMS

HAT(S):
Baseball caps are good but I prefer the fully foldable ones with an all-round brim which give better sun and wind protection.

SARONGS/SARAPES/WRAPS:
These are essential in places where the culture is to cover up. If trekking or hiking, you can get someone to hold them up for you as a barricade if you need to go to the loo when there isn't a tree to be seen! Wear to the water's edge at beaches where covering up is preferable but you want to swim. They also do double-duty as head scarf/hair cover in warmer climates (just like the pashmina). And as a stand-by extra, they make great sheets and line dodgy mattresses.

SMALL ALARM CLOCK:
For those early morning flights!

SMALL CALCULATOR:
So handy. Practice converting your dollar into different currencies and get to know what the 'trend' with a currency has been to see if it will move in your favor or not when you travel. The more you get used to doing it the better your money tracking record will be. You can then work out whether you can afford to stay in a slightly better place or if you have enough spare cash to buy that small Buddha statue in Kathmandu.

WATERPROOF PONCHO:

These are available at disposal stores and they are incredibly handy. They are made of clear plastic and come in a small pack that you can keep in your day-pack or camera bag. In addition you can wear your backpack underneath so if it rains, your gear won't get soggy, and you won't have to turn back and miss anything.

SALWAR KAMEEZ:

Long-sleeved tunic and pants combination that is perfect in Asian countries, some parts of Africa and the Middle East. Covers skin appropriately and is comfortable to travel in.

BOARD SHORTS AND LONG-SLEEVED RASH VEST:

Great for surfing, modest beach swimming and also really good for sun protection (plus they double as daytime wear).

BLACK TRENCH COAT:

Fantastic to dress up a pair of jeans. Layer underneath with sweaters for a wind-breaker that doesn't take up as much room as a normal heavy winter coat. Wear with boots and good earrings for a stylish city sightseeing look.

... AND WHAT TO UNPACK!

Unpack anything that you don't really like, that doesn't fit properly, that you haven't worn before or that you wore once and never again. Don't pack it because you think it might be useful for something. It won't. Not only that, you'll regret lugging it everywhere. Also ditch:

• **Anything that comes in glass cases or bottles** or is best left on the bathroom shelf.
• Put the glittery, **overtly trendy clothing items back in the wardrobe** until you return.
• **Ditto the platform evening shoes**. You can always buy something frivolous when you're away if you get desperate for a fashion fix.
• **Trim the makeup bag down to basics**: tweezers, small nail scissors, lip balm or gloss, mascara, concealer (for those extracurricular pimples!).
• You don't need eye shadows, blushers, lipsticks and eyeliners, etc. Truly.
• **Super-heavy books and magazines**.
• **HUGE shampoos, conditioners and other hair products**. Decant into small travel bottles and resign yourself to the fact that your hair will be OK without them even if you run out towards the end of your trip.
• **Five sweaters – you will only need one or two at the most**.

Be a bit ruthless!

REPEAT AFTER ME:
I WILL UNPACK ANYTHING THAT IS NOT PRACTICAL OR THAT I WILL NEVER WEAR!

111

HEALTH MATTERS

Good health is the crucial ingredient to successful and happy travels. Ideally you should see your family doctor or a general practitioner in the planning stages of your trip and then again - just before you go - to get the all-clear for your health. Any specific requirements you may have for your personal wellbeing can then be addressed in good time and with all the information up front.

Visit the Travel Doctor's website [See page 242 for this link]. They do a fantastic booklet which contains valuable info about altitude sickness (for trekking and hiking) as well as general medical stuff regarding infectious diseases, such as typhoid and malaria. **Read up on the symptoms of the major health problems so you can recognize them in yourself and others if need be.** There is also a comprehensive list of everything you need for a good medical kit.

Obtain a prescription for broad spectrum antibiotics and take these with you as well as general tablets and remedies for diarrhea and

tummy problems. Pack water purifying iodine tablets if you're hiking or trekking in wilderness areas. Be sure to include basic Band-Aids (you'll need them for blisters!), gauze and antiseptic cream. Even though it will probably seem quite bulky, **the best thing that can happen is that you drag it all over the world and never have to use it**. That's you triumphant at the summit ... ha!

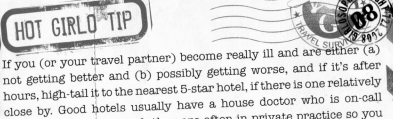

HOT GIRLO TIP

If you (or your travel partner) become really ill and are either (a) not getting better and (b) possibly getting worse, and if it's after hours, high-tail it to the nearest 5-star hotel, if there is one relatively close by. Good hotels usually have a house doctor who is on-call 24-7 for guests, although they are often in private practice so you could possibly even telephone them, once you have their details. These doctors are really well regarded and usually experienced in diagnosing and treating travel illnesses. Don't delay! The sooner you get a diagnosis the sooner you'll be in recovery and able to keep on rolling!

WHAT'S IN GIRLO'S MEDICAL KIT?

It's always the pharmacy stuff that takes up the most space in a bag. **And often a lot of it doesn't get used but this stuff is critical.** In a health crisis clothes aren't so important. You can always make do.

But here are a few must-have items for your medical kit:

+ MOSQUITO REPELLANT:
Approaching sunset in mosquito-prone climates and areas (especially where malaria is a known problem), this stuff, whether as a roll-on or spray, is a must!

+ PLENTY OF TAMPONS:
Sometimes these are not available in remote locations (thick sanitary pads are no fun when you're trekking).

+ PANTY-LINERS:
These are great for a long day of traveling and in conditions when you will be without a shower for a time. Think: overnight train trips, car rides through desert regions.

+ WET WIPES:
For face, hands and general hygiene while you're on the road.

+ ANTIBACTERIAL HANDY WIPES:
My absolute essential for hands, especially before eating anything.

+ TEA TREE OIL:
The natural antiseptic for cuts and small grazes.

+ ARNICA:
The remedy for bruises, sprains and muscle aches. Use the cream plus the homeopathic tablets that go under the tongue as a fast-track method to reduce swelling and pain from bruising injuries. Apply as soon as possible after injury for best results.

SHHH
HOT G
SECRE

+ ECHINACEA:

Immune system drops; just 15 to 20 drops in juice or bottled water three times a day at the onset of cold or flu will do the trick. Do this for 3 to 4 days or until symptoms fade.

+ GASTROLYTE POWDER:

For tummy upsets. Great for replacing electrolytes if you get Delhi Belly ... or Beirut Belly! Add to bottled water and drink 2 to 3 times daily.

+ COTTON BUDS:

Useful for general personal and medical care.

+ SUNSCREEN:

This is really something you must never be without. Go for SPF 30+ and a water-resistant gel-style sunscreen (the creamy ones can be a bit pore-clogging).

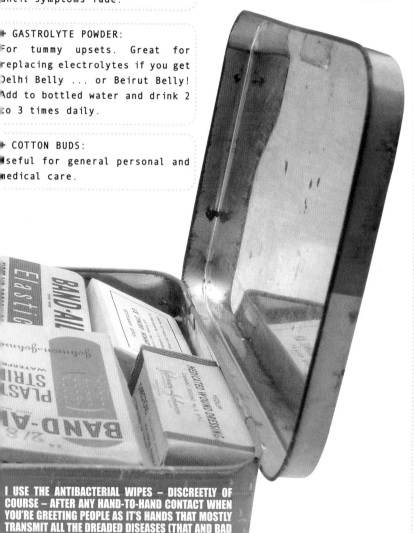

I USE THE ANTIBACTERIAL WIPES — DISCREETLY OF COURSE — AFTER ANY HAND-TO-HAND CONTACT WHEN YOU'RE GREETING PEOPLE AS IT'S HANDS THAT MOSTLY TRANSMIT ALL THE DREADED DISEASES (THAT AND BAD WATER SUPPLIES!).

DON'T SPECULATE, VACCINATE!

You should always check a few months in advance what vaccinations and medical precautions are necessary for the countries you are entering before you travel. In addition, you should keep your immunization certificate in your passport hold-all, sometimes customs ask to see these, and also you will then be more conscious of when you need to update your immunity. Some vaccines are for

life (Hepatitis B) but some (like Tetanus) should be renewed every ten years to be effective; possibly more frequently if you're in contact with animals or building things in remote areas (rusty nails and old building supplies can cause infection which can be life threatening). **Check with a doctor before you leave and be a pincushion for a short time ...**

IT MAY SAVE YOUR LIFE.

WHAT'S IN THE BANK?

From time to time you should check in with your savings plan to make sure you're on point. How are you going? Have you met your target? If not, how are you going to make up the shortfall?

If you have a birthday on the near horizon or if Christmas is coming, perhaps you could put the word out to everyone that they can 'donate' a small amount to your trip instead of buying you a gift. Maybe there is an opportunity to step up your part-time hours at your job? Or is there another way you could earn pocket money at home – wash your parents' or the neighbor's car, the family dog or do the garden?

The more you are able to take, the greater the freedom once you're away. There is nothing worse than traveling somewhere and not having the money to actually participate in the things that make that particular place what it is.

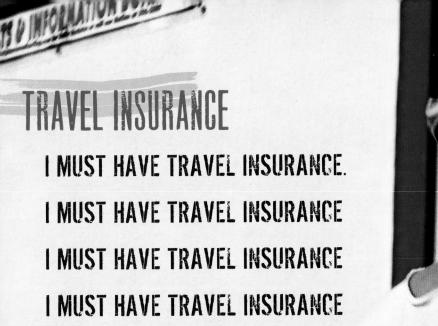

TRAVEL INSURANCE

I MUST HAVE TRAVEL INSURANCE.

I MUST HAVE TRAVEL INSURANCE

I MUST HAVE TRAVEL INSURANCE

I MUST HAVE TRAVEL INSURANCE

DO NOT LEAVE HOME WITHOUT IT AND
DON'T STAY AWAY WITHOUT UPDATING IT!

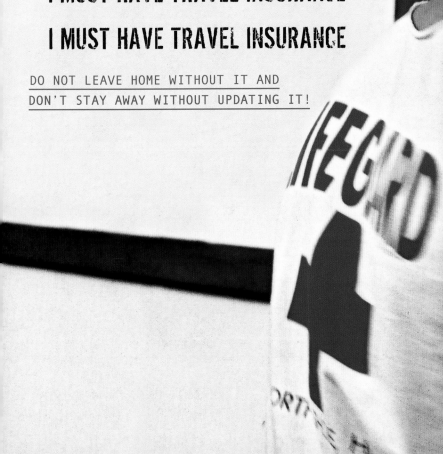

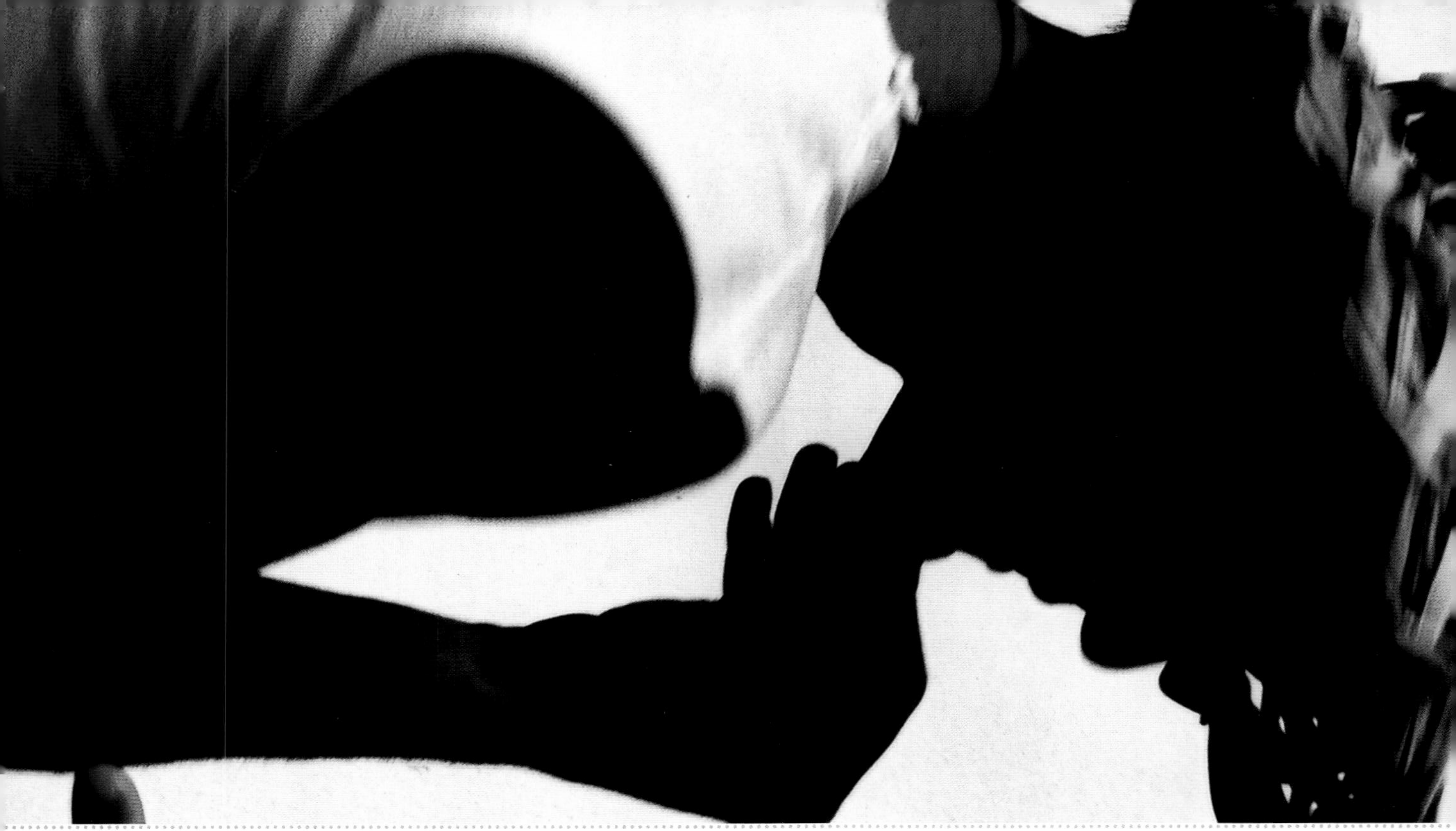

WORKING
OVERSEAS/INTERSTATE

If you want to work your way around the world, you'll
have to become savvy in the visa application and resume
process. **If you can spring it, this is a fantastic way
to really live and work long-term in another country and
perhaps use the base you create for further traveling
opportunities**. But it's all about the paperwork! Many
companies are keen to employ people with the right
background, skills and education, and the recruitment
process is often the same as for a normal job.

Typically companies who sponsor recruits from other countries have a system for doing so and this means they organize the visa for you, which is a bonus.

But don't disregard the job market closer to home either - working interstate can perhaps get you closer to an international airport that allows you to do more traveling and more cheaply too. Perhaps you need to move to another coast!

TRAINING: PREPARE THE VESSEL!

Fitness should be a part of everyone's life-management strategy but where health and fitness really pays off is when you are traveling. Not only will you endure long-haul trips and flights more readily, **you'll arrive in better condition** if you have good fitness and muscle tone. In addition, **you'll recover better in new time zones and you will bounce back from even small illnesses**. Being fit means you have more stamina to do more things in general once you're away. **Lifting and carrying luggage is easier**, as is loading up cars, and walking to see the sights (think steps of The Acropolis in Greece and Sigirya of Sri Lanka or the long walk to Machu Picchu in Peru).

If you are going away to do a sport, such as surfing, snowboarding, skiing or sailing, you should prepare according to the needs of that activity. **Don't be unprepared physically for a trip that requires you to be in form!** Consult websites that are relevant

for specific sports training or ask an expert to help you design a program so you'll get the most out of your trip.

If you are trekking, hiking or mountain climbing, you should do the research on what to expect. Altitude training may be essential and you need to know how altitudes can affect you. It is not uncommon to get altitude sickness even if you're lower than the base camp of Everest (which by the way is 5500 meters or 18,000 feet). You can become affected by altitude at around 2400 meters above sea level. That's about 8000 feet. **So be aware of your geography and topography and how your body may be affected.**

BEFORE YOU LEAVE:

- EMBARK ON A PROGRAM OF WALKING, RUNNING, SWIMMING AND WEIGHTS.
- TAKE THE DOG ALONG WHEN YOU WALK OR GO CYCLING.
- DO YOGA AND PILATES FOR FLEXIBILITY AND CORE STRENGTH.
- RUN IN SOFT SAND ON THE BEACH.
- DO SIT-UPS – LOTS OF THEM – TO STRENGTHEN YOUR BACK AND STOMACH FOR ALL THAT BACKPACK AND BAG LIFTING YOU'LL BE DOING WHILE YOU'RE AWAY.

RELATIONSHIPS & EXPECTATIONS

This is included in this section because you will need to give family, friends and/or your significant other some sort of fair notice of your impending departure.

With a serious romantic relationship, tread delicately and discuss your feelings and reasons for going. If the other person has no plans to join you (or if in fact you haven't invited them to) you should at least talk through your reasons. If you want the relationship to continue upon your return, talk about this too. Know however that this may be a big ask, especially if you are planning to be away for a long period of time. **Be fair and be aware too that there are some things that are better left unsaid**. If you want them to propose marriage or something more permanent but you know in your heart they are not ready or the two of you are too young then don't bring it up, as it will probably only confuse things at a time when you have already made some clear decisions.

BE BRAVE AND KNOW THAT IF YOU FOLLOW YOUR HEART
WHATEVER HAPPENS IS FOR THE BEST.

Regarding your family and friends, **you should have open, clear and honest discussions** about what you expect will happen while you're away. If you have a pet, who in the family can look after it for you? If you have other things such as boats and cars that need to have the motor turned over, or the vehicle re-registered, mail to be collected or papers to be lodged at certain times, or even banking matters to be attended to, make sure they are happy to assist you. **Ensure that you won't be putting a burden on anyone while you're gone**.

If you have flatmates or rent your accommodation then you will need to give advance notice to the people whom you live with or to the landlord directly if it's your lease. Be fair and try not to leave anyone in a hole or struggling financially. Make sure that you do your bit to 'do the right thing' by all concerned.

Organize storage for your personal stuff either off site or – if you are planning to return to the same place – in a secure, agreed upon location within the house or garage, etc. Leave enough time to pack things up, thoroughly clean your room, and to dispose of any rubbish, unwanted items and so on, well ahead of time. Giving those who will be affected by your plans as much notice as you can will make it easier for all concerned and ensure you don't lose either a friendship – or a bond!

HOLIDAY PRACTICE (A WEEK AWAY!)

If you have planned to go trekking, a practice trip beforehand is in order. No matter how easy the brochures might make it look, it's guaranteed to be harder! Consult the group or tour guide to see if they can recommend any specific local treks or nearby walking tours that will help you to prepare for your big trip. **It will help you to train for packing, carrying and organizing yourself.** Sometimes all you need is a small trip to find out your weak spots! Use this week away to refine and address your traveling weaknesses. It won't solve every issue but **it will definitely help you when you get into the Big League**.

"YOU CANNOT **PREPARE** FOR EVERY PROBLEM T H A T MAY **ARISE** ON THE **ROAD.** A L L **YOU** CAN **DO** IS H A V E THE **GRACE** TO WORK T H R O U G H THE **SITUATION** THAT **PRESENTS.**"

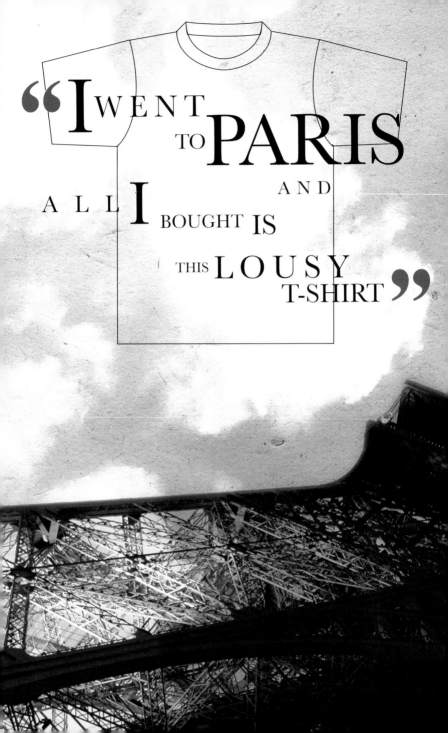

"**I** WENT TO **PARIS** AND ALL **I** BOUGHT IS THIS **LOUSY** T-SHIRT"

131

CHAPTER 4
DEPARTURES

RALPH WALDO EMERSON

66

THOUGH WE TRAVEL THE WORLD OVER TO FIND THE BEAUTIFUL, WE MUST CARRY IT WITH US OR WE WILL NOT FIND IT.

RALPH WALDO EMERSON

99

Sweet sorrow or joyful tomorrow? **Parting or leaving affects each of us differently**. When you are going on a journey, adventure or new path, the physical act of leaving can be emotional, even traumatic.

The word 'leaving' contains in it the implication of something or someone and a sense of movement away from them. This sense of what is being left behind can make a parting seem loaded. **It can be painful or it can be positive and joyful. It is up to each traveler to decide how to cope and process it**.

Someone may prefer not to say anything at the time of departure, others use it as a moment to reconnect. **However it is done, it is best done briefly**. Drawn-out farewells can get tiring and they increase the emotional content more than may be necessary or appropriate. Control the scene and control your response to it. **Decide that you will be happy, even though there will be some sadness at the time**. Prepare for it ahead of time – you know it will be a matter of weeks, months or even years perhaps, but take the attitude that you will be seeing everyone again.

IT'S JUST ANOTHER TIME ZONE!

"IT CAN BE PAINFUL OR IT CAN BE POSITIVE AND JOYFUL.

IT IS UP TO EACH TRAVELER TO DECIDE HOW TO COPE AND PROCESS IT."

PTER 4

YOUR EXIT STRATEGY

Once you have packed your bags (the ones you are taking with you!), put them neatly in a corner of your room or flat. Then survey your immediate environment. What state is it in? Have you destroyed the room in the process of packing? Chances are it could do with a bit of a rearrange, scrub and a clear-out before you go, even if it's just your bedroom. **Just because you're leaving it doesn't mean you should leave a total mess for everyone else to clean up. Your parents or flatmates will be thoroughly appreciative (if a little shocked!) by your mature approach to your exit strategy.**

What about the things you're not taking? Have you got any leftover items in your clothing storage space? Do you still need them? Can they be given to a charity? **Create a bag of unwanted clothing and clear out the things you won't wear again. Be ruthless!** You are bound to buy things that will be more up-to-date while you're away on your trip.

Put away spare pillows and bedding in the linen cupboard. Then, change the sheets on your bed. You'll probably be excited about what lies ahead but also you may be tired from all the preparations, so **make your last night in your own bed a fresh, comfortable one** so you get some sort of sleep and you're not over-tired for your travels.

CLEAN SWEEP

Leave yourself the rest of the day to simply clean, sort and pare down your personal world. A few tips:

TUPPERWARE RULES:
Put all paperwork, files, school and study stuff in a Tupperware container with the lid on. These are wonderful for stacking, and ensure that you'll be able to put your hands on things once you get back. **You don't want things going astray while you're gone, so put them away!**

WARDROBE:
Use any spare plastic garment protectors from the dry cleaner to hang up anything that's without a drawer or basket. Put any items hanging on the back of the door away in the wardrobe.

PAPER TOWELS:
Use these to wipe down all the surfaces on desks, bedside tables and clean mirrors and window sills.

SORT OUT YOUR CHEST OF DRAWERS:
You never know if you might need Mom to send over some of your things so at least make it easy for her to find them!

VACCUM:
Get in under the bed and all around the room and dust off bookshelves.

BOX SHOES:
Then stack away in a cupboard if you are not going to take them with you.

FINAL CHECKLIST

on the LASt Night Before or Morning of DePArtUre:

• CALL friends AND fAMiLY, AND SAY GooDBYe, AND while You're tALKiNG to them DoUBLe-CheCK their eMAIL AND PoStAL ADDreSSes.

• tAKe VitAMiNS AND eChiNACeA So YoUr iMMUNe SYStem StAYS StroNG - LeAViNG CAN Be StreSSfUL AND it CAN MAKe YoU A Bit 'rUN DoWN' if YoU DoN't tAKe PreCAUtions.

• eAt heALthY SiMPLe fooD ALL DAY So YoU DoN't Get on the PLANe or trAin feeLiNG BLoAteD AND UNCoMfortABLe.

• CheCK YoUr hAND BAGGAGe hAS YoUr itiNerArY, tiCKetS, PASSPortS AND ViSAS ALL iN A SAfe, Yet eASY-to-ACCeSS PortfoLio or hoLD-ALL.

• ChArGe YoUr iPoD - DoN't LeAVe home withoUt A fULL BAtterY.

• CheCK YoU hAVe the CorreCt PoWer ADAPtorS for the firSt CoUNtrieS YoU Are ViSitiNG iN YoUr hAND LUGGAGe.

• CheCK LABeLS AND LUGGAGe tAGS Are CLeAr, LeGiBLe AND ContAiN YoUr home ADDreSS AND DetAiLS.

• ADD CoLorfUL LUGGAGe riBBoNS or StrAPS for eASY iDeNtifiCAtion At the other eND.

• ChArGe YoUr BLACKBerrY or LAPtoP if YoU're trAVeLiNG with them.

• CheCK YoUr Lift to the Airport or trAiN StAtion iS ALL Set AND ArriViNG AheAD of time So YoU hAVe A Bit to SPAre from the StArt.

• reConfirm YoUr fLiGht (or trAin or BUS) AND the DePArtUre time.

• reCheCK whiCh terMiNAL At the DePArtUre PoiNt YoU wiLL Be CheCKiNG iN At.

• trAVeL iNSUrANCe? MAKe SUre YoU hAVe it UP-to-DAte AND SUffiCieNt CoVerAGe.

• LAY oUt trAVeL CLotheS AND ACCeSSorieS for the next DAY.

• PAre DoWN CoSMetiCS AND BAthroom StUff into A SMALLer BAG.

• DoN't forGet to LeAVe oUt YoUr toothBrUSh AND toothPAStE for the MorNiNG, AND then DoN't forGet to PACK them!

WHAT TO WEAR WHEN TRAVELING

You will have already put some thought into what you will wear on the plane and while you are traveling in general. **If you dress up a bit to travel it seems to make your passage that much smoother**. Check-in staff will smile a bit brighter, the all-important customs and security people seem to be more cordial, flight attendants don't mind to go the extra mile for that blanket or drink that you need. **When you appear well groomed and crisply turned out, even if you are only wearing jeans and a nice shirt – it speaks volumes**. When you appear disheveled and sloppy, it sends the message that you don't really care and you can't really cope. A good basic outfit consists of:

- WELL-CUT, CLEAN, COMFY JEANS/PANTS (NOT SUPER-TIGHT!).
- CRSIP, PLAIN-COLORED COTTON SHORT- OR LONG-SLEEVED T.
- SWEATER OR PASHMINA DRAPED AROUND NECK OR SHOULDERS.
- GOOD, SIMPLE EARRINGS AND WATCH.
- MINIMAL MAKEUP AND FRESHLY WASHED HAIR, CLIPPED BACK OR TIED UP IN A PONYTAIL.
- NEW TRAINERS OR NICE FLAT WALKING BOOTS.

AND WHAT NOT TO WEAR

- TRACKSUITS.
- T-SHIRTS WITH INAPPROPRIATE MESSAGES OR OBSCENITIES.
- G-STRINGS (YOU BEND OVER A LOT WHEN YOU TRAVEL AND THESE ALWAYS RIDE UP).
- ALL UNDERWEAR THAT IS TRYING TO BE OUTERWEAR (AND SHOULDN'T BE).
- MESSY, EXTREME-COLORED HAIR (ONLY BECAUSE IT MAY SINGLE YOU OUT FOR EXTRA ATTENTION BY CUSTOMS AND JUST IN GENERAL, WHICH MAY NOT BE TO YOUR ADVANTAGE).
- DIRTY, MUDDY TRAINERS (QUARANTINE OFFICERS ARE ALWAYS INTERESTED IN MUD).
- TOO MUCH CHEAP JEWELRY.
- TONS OF MAKEUP.

TO BE A GOOD TRAVELER, YOU FLY UNDER THE RADAR. DRESSING QUIETLY BUT WELL IS A GOOD HABIT, DRAWING NOTHING, EXCEPT THE ATTENTION YOU WANT.

AND SO TO BED... EARLY

Getting a good night's sleep before you travel is sometimes hard but really great if you can manage it. Staying up all night before you go, saying goodbyes and partying, is not sensible. If you prepare and count down your time properly, you'll probably be tired anyway. Hopefully with all your stuff packed and your clothes for the morning laid out, you'll be ready to **hop into bed early the night before with a herbal tea and a good book**. That's the smart way to go!

> "THE REAL VOYAGE OF DISCOVERY CONSISTS NOT IN SEEKING NEW LANDSCAPES BUT IN HAVING NEW EYES."
>
> MARCEL PROUST

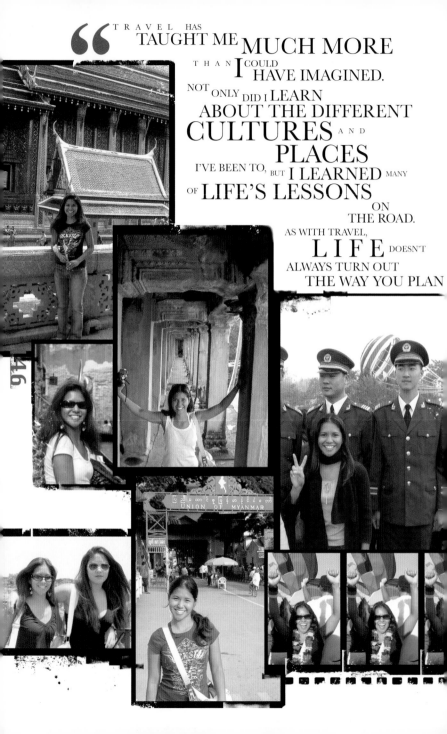

TRAVEL HAS TAUGHT ME MUCH MORE THAN I COULD HAVE IMAGINED. NOT ONLY DID I LEARN ABOUT THE DIFFERENT CULTURES AND PLACES I'VE BEEN TO, BUT I LEARNED MANY OF LIFE'S LESSONS ON THE ROAD. AS WITH TRAVEL, LIFE DOESN'T ALWAYS TURN OUT THE WAY YOU PLAN

YOU GOTTA OVERCOME OBSTACLES, LEARN TO ADAPT, DEAL WITH THE UNEXPECTED, ACCEPT AND CHANGE.

ON THE ROAD, I'VE ALSO LEARNED MORE ABOUT MYSELF AND WHO I AM AS A YOUNG WOMAN IN THIS WORLD.

MY ADVICE TO OTHER TRAVELERS IS TO BE OPENMINDED, RESPECTFUL, AND HAVE A GREAT SENSE OF HUMOR!

I ENJOY ANTHONY BOURDAIN'S QUOTE 'BE A TRAVELER, NOT A TOURIST'.

JONI CAMINOS
GIRLOSOPHER
HAWAII

CHAPTER 5
IN TRANSIT

IN JANUARY 2006, MY BOYFRIEND ASHTON AND I TRAVELED TO TRUJILLO, PERU, TO VOLUNTEER WITH STREET KIDS IN OUR UNIVERSITY HOLIDAYS. WE VOLUNTEERED WITH A PERUVIAN NGO CALLED 'AWAITING ANGELS', WHICH PLACED US IN TRUJILLO CEMETERY TO WORK WITH THE CHILDREN WHO CLEAN GRAVES AND REPLACE FLOWERS IN THE CEMETERY DAILY. THEY DO THIS IN EXCHANGE FOR TIPS FROM VISITORS. AFTER OUR MONTH OF VOLUNTEERING WE SPENT A WEEK TRAVELING THROUGH CUSCO AND THE SACRED VALLEY.

It was an amazing experience, but also challenging. As do all trips to developing countries, the experience made me realize how much we take for granted in Australia. Widespread access to adequate housing, a supportive social welfare system and a relatively progressive level of equality between the sexes are all aspects of Western society that really enhance our quality of life.

I definitely saw first-hand how the lack of these things affect the psychological and physical health of individuals in developing countries. Nevertheless the children we worked with were beautiful kids, often very selfless and always protective and loyal, despite the hardships they endured on a daily basis.

They taught me so much and they will always hold a special place in my heart

SIMONE KING
VOLUNTEER, GIRLOSOPHER, STUDENT

THE GIRLO TRAVEL SURVIVAL KIT

SIMONE KING
VOLUNTEER
GIRLOSOPHER

PAGE #   149

CHAPTER #   5

CHAPTER   IN TRANSIT

IN THE 'DROP-OFF' ZONE

Airports, railway stations and bus depots are crowded places at the best of times. Arriving for an early departure, dealing with your baggage, check-in lines and meeting up with your travel companion(s) and/or family and friends who are there to see you off, can be daunting. **Having a strategy to navigate these somewhat chaotic public spaces is a sound policy when you travel.**

Invariably the drop-off is tricky, because airports are often being upgraded and they seem to change a lot, which can make finding things that much harder. Not only that the security staff will shoo cars away after a few minutes of being parked so **you will need to have a streamlined approach** so you don't become rattled at the beginning of it all.

Get a map of the terminal or station off the internet or use a local street map to work out your entrance and exit points. **Locate specifically where your check-in will be for your airline** (they each have their own) so you can have Dad or Aunt Sally pull up in the car as close as possible to offload you and your gear before they go and park. **Using a taxi is usually a bit easier as the cabbies mostly have this information wired.**

TROLLEY DOLLY

Many airports have free trolleys but lots don't. Keep coins handy so you can access them easily. Load up with the biggest bag on the bottom (pack it flat-side down), stacking the smaller bags on top.

If you are taking sporting items, such as surfboards in surfboard bags or snowboarding gear, etc., then you should carry these over your shoulder (padded shoulder straps are a must). That way you can keep both hands on the trolley for steering straight. If you have a small daypack, computer or handbag, place it in the basket of the trolley.

Using a trolley makes moving around the airport easier and you won't be exhausted by trailing your gear around.

GET ONE!

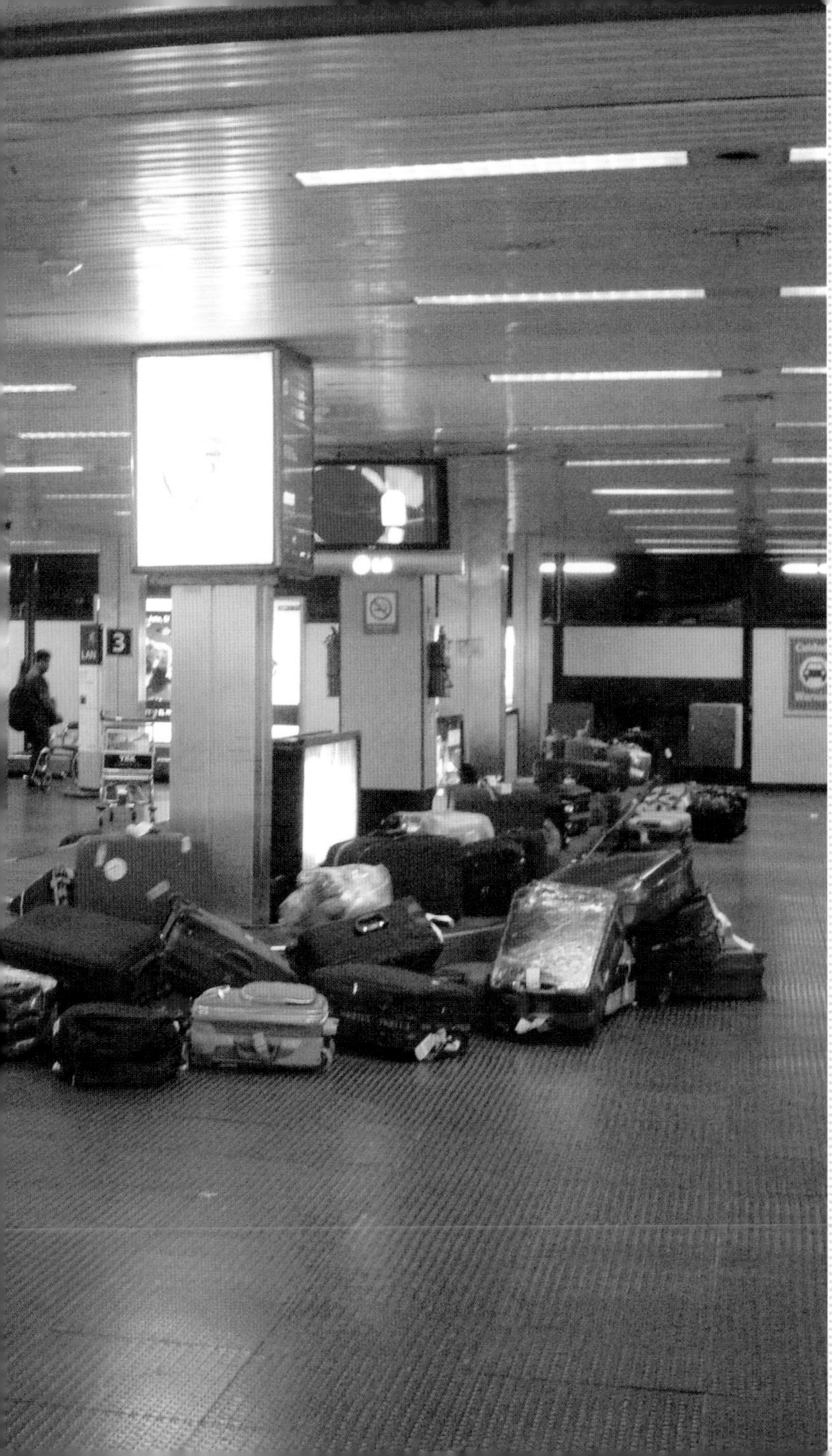
3

THE CHECK-IN

Go to the big video screens inside the terminal
and look for your flight number. Next to it will
say which check-in (numbered desk) you go to.
**Once you've located it, double-check you're in
the right line**. There's nothing worse than waiting
in a line only to discover that you're waiting in
the wrong spot or that the line you're in actually
snakes around the corner to another check-in
desk!

While you're waiting in line, fill in the airline luggage tags for each piece of luggage including your hand luggage. Even though you will already have your own, these ones are added protection and link your luggage to your airline, which will make it easier to ensure they don't go astray. You might also have to fill in departure forms, etc., depending on your country of departure. This might be a good time to do those as well.

SECURITY - THE NEW WORLD ORDER

Once you have checked in you will receive your boarding pass with the departure gate on it and your seat allocation. Now you have to pass through the security check-point to access customs and immigration. It is a not-so-brave world these days. Everyone is scared and therefore extremely cautious about terrorism. It's a fact of life if you're traveling anywhere, and we all must endure it for the foreseeable future.

The trick is to be ready and one step ahead of the game so that it doesn't get you rattled and feeling spread out and disorganized as you split up all your personal bits and pieces to go through the walk-through barrier and the X-ray machines. Here are some basic security reminders:

Your Shoes: these DAYS You need to remove them for AN inspection BY the AirPort SeCUritY.

MetALLiC oBJeCts: BeLts AnD ANYthinG SUCh AS JeweLrY, hAir ACCeSSories, wAtCheS, MoBiLe PhoneS ALL Get SCAnneD AnD neeD to Be PUt in the SePArAte trAYS then PLACeD on A ConVeYor BeLt thAt GoeS throUGh the X-rAY MAChine. YoU CoLLeCt them At the other enD.

COAts: tAKe these off AnD PLACe them in SePArAte trAYS AS weLL.

LAptop CoMPUterS: remoVe it from YoUr CoMPUter BAG, PLACe in the trAY ProViDeD AnD SenD Both BAG AnD trAY throUGh the X-rAY. SoMetiMeS YoU wiLL Be ASKeD to remoVe the BAtterY.

i hAVe eVen Been ASKeD to fire UP the CoMPUter So SeCUritY CoULD oBSerVe it wAS workinG.

CAMerAS: these ALSo Go on A trAY AnD throUGh the X-rAY.

fiLM: thiS iS A toUGh one   - SoMetiMeS theY CAn hAnD-CheCk it for YoU BUt MoStLY theY wiLL inSiSt it GoeS throUGh the X-rAY. MoSt X-rAYS wiLL StAte whether theY Are fiLM SAfe. UnLeSS YoU Are A ProfeSSionAL PhotoGrAPher it's USUALLY wiSer to PUt the fiLM throUGh with ALL YoUr other iteMS. DiGitAL CAMerAS Are the oBVioUS SoLUtion to thiS ProBLeM.

hAnD BAGS / hAnD LUGGAGe: PLACe these fLAt on the BeLt to Go throUGh X-rAY.

DrinKS: DUe to new SeCUritY MeASUreS At AirPortS YoU MAY Be ASKeD to DrinK from AnY BottLe YoU Are CArrYinG to ProVe it's not SoMethinG eLSe.

CoSMetiCS: MAnY AirLineS Are ASKinG for ALL CoSMetiCS AnD PerSonAL CAre iteMS to Be PLACeD in trAnSPArent ZiP-LoCK BAGS to Go throUGh SeCUritY. in ADDition theY reQUire thAt no inDiViDUAL iteM ContAin More thAn 100 MiLLiLiterS (3.5 fL oZ) of fLUiD or CreAM. CheCK the LABeLS. if in DoUBt: ASK. Be AwAre thAt if YoU trY to Get SoMethinG throUGh thAt iS forBiDDen theY CAn throw the iteM oUt AnD YoU MAY eVen Be BAnneD from BoArDinG the PLAne.

YoU CoULD ALSo Be inDefiniteLY DetAineD AnD therefore YoU CAn Be in A DiffiCULt SitUAtion. Don't riSK it.

ShArP oBJeCtS: tweeZerS, rAZorS, PoCKet KniVeS AnD nAiL SCiSSorS hAVe Been ConfiSCAteD At PrActiCALLY eVerY AirPort in the worLD SinCe the new SeCUritY MeASUreS CAMe in. PACK ALL ShArP oBJeCtS in YoUr MAin BAG or hAVe theM Join the other 100,000 thAt were SePArAteD from their UnhAPPY ownerS.

note: AS SeCUritY MeASUreS Are ChAnGinG ALL the tiMe, YoU ShoULD CheCK with the AirLine Before YoU fLY So YoU Know the LAteSt MeASUreS AnD whAt to exPeCt.

HOT GIRLO TIP

Count your hand luggage pieces and trays before you step through security. Try to load things onto the conveyor belt for the X-ray as you step through the metal detector so you all arrive on the other side at roughly the same time. This is hard if the person in front hasn't removed their belt or watch! Put your shoes back on first. Recount your trays and items. Ask for help from the security staff if you feel unable to gather all your things.

SAYING GOODBYE

Before you get to customs and immigration you need to do your farewells. Say goodbye with a tear and a smile – it's a joyous time for you and a time to be proud too! Your family will be sad but also excited for you and your friends will miss you. But this is a new beginning – it's all about anticipation and potential – which means looking forward not backwards!

You should know that your family will have concerns that you'll be safe and sound so make it a policy to check in with them as often as you can or as often as you can afford to while you are away. They worry because they love you, not because they don't trust you! Reassure them that you are well-prepared (you are!) and that you'll contact them on arrival, just to let them know you got there safely. Which, of course, is both caring and thoughtful. And which of course, you are.

CUSTOMS AND IMMIGRATION

You're there ... well, almost. You'll need to go through customs and immigration checkpoints. Depending on where you are departing, you'll need to fill in some forms, and answer questions. A lot of this you will have learned about during your preparation for your trip. Answer questions on any immigration forms as accurately as possible. Paperwork is a fact of traveling and while it takes some getting used to, doing it efficiently and honestly is part of the deal!

KNOW YOUR PASSPORT NUMBER –
LEARN IT OFF BY HEART!

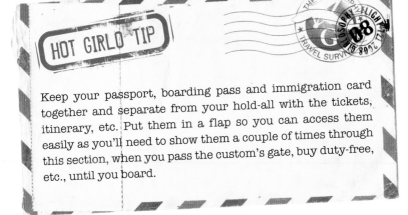

HOT GIRLO TIP

Keep your passport, boarding pass and immigration card together and separate from your hold-all with the tickets, itinerary, etc. Put them in a flap so you can access them easily as you'll need to show them a couple of times through this section, when you pass the custom's gate, buy duty-free, etc., until you board.

CAMERA FILM CORNER

ALL BATTERY, VIDEO CASSETTES, DIGITAL FILM SOLD HERE.

CAMERA
FILM CORNER

LAST-MINUTE SHOPPING

It's only OK to do shopping at the airport if you have forgotten or truly need something! One guilt-free way to shop is to buy small gifts from your country of origin that will fit into your daypack to give to children or to give as gifts to your driver or to a guide. In some countries (especially in Asia) gift giving is both ritual and customary. In certain places you give a present when you arrive as a greeting or as a departing gesture. Even shopkeepers sometimes give things to you (which can get confusing but usually when you're being a 'good' customer and spending!). **Small souvenir-type gifts will always be greatly appreciated.**

It's tempting to go nuts at the duty-free shops ... but you don't really need to buy tons of cosmetics or gadgets even if you save a bit of money. It's just more stuff to carry and very often a false economy if you don't normally buy luxury items! **My golden rule for duty-free shopping is this: I allow myself to buy something only if it's a gift for whoever meets me at the other end** – meaning it's an object to carry short-term. Or, if I'm coming home I buy perfume for my mother or some aftershave for my father, so again it's offloaded quickly.

DUTY-FREE IS FOR DIEHARD SHOPPERS
NOT DIEHARD TRAVELERS!

SAFETY FIRST

Now that you are near the point of departure, **it's time to review safety consciousness** for the time you will be away. Basically the normal rules of safety apply exactly as they do at home. You wouldn't walk down a dark alley in any city so don't do it when you're away. You wouldn't accept a lift or an invitation from a stranger, nor attend a party where you are not sure how you'll get home. Same applies overseas.

YOU DON'T NEED TO BE PARANOID –
THIS LIST IS NOT MEANT TO MAKE YOU FEARFUL,
IT'S TO HELP YOU DEVELOP AWARENESS.

**After a while doing this stuff will become second
nature** and you'll be on top of things at all
times. It's quite true that there's no place
like home, where you may even leave the doors
unlocked and it's all fairly relaxed, however,
you're about to leave the nest ...

- Stick with your travel companion.
  There is safety in numbers.

- Always keep an eye on your bags and never
  leave them unattended, not even for a second.
  This is a rule at airports and train stations anyway.

- Do not leave all your baggage and gear in a
  locked car anywhere.

- Make a pact with your traveling companion to
  watch out for each other's gear. Know how many
  pieces of luggage you are traveling with and
  keep count of them. Recount at every unloading
  and reloading. Watch each other's back(pack)!

- Pickpockets are professionals and they work in
  teams. They also work in public places where there
  are a lot of people. Wear your day pack on your
  front or have padlocks on every pocket. Keep your
  eyes peeled and be aware of who is around you.

- Handbags, even in urban centers, should be worn
  over one shoulder and the strap held securely
  with your other arm so it's hard for someone to
  yank it off.

- If you stop to have a bite to eat and you are on
  the road with a car, bus or van full of gear, get
  take-out or park the car where you can clearly
  see it, unless someone is staying with the vehicle.

- When you are traveling in a car or mini-van, lock
  all doors from the inside (you may have to do this
  yourself if the car is an old clunker).

- Ensure when you hire a taxi, it is a legal one.
  Some places operate an illegal cab service which

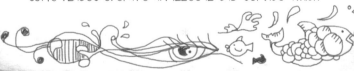

LoCALS MAY USE BUt it norMALLY MeAnS UnLiCensed AnD UnreGistered DriVerS. if YoU hAVe An ACCiDent in one of theSe, YoU MAY rUn into inSUrAnCe ProBLemS LAter.

- MAKe SUre YoU ALWAYS tAKe Both KeYS to the room when YoU Go oUt for the DAY.

- Be PrUDent with the informAtion YoU GiVe oUt, howeVer, Be PoLite AnD frienDLY – YoU'LL Be ASKeD A ZiLLion timeS 'exCUSe Me, MiSS, whAt CoUntrY YoU Come from?' YoU CAn CertAinLY SmiLe AnD Let them Know BUt thAt DoeSn't MeAn YoU neeD to teLL them YoUr Life StorY!

- Be eSPeCiALLY CArefUL not to reVeAL where YoU Are StAYinG, nor whAt YoUr trAVeL PLANS Are to JUSt AnYone. thiS iS DoUBLY imPortAnt if YoU Are trAVeLinG ALone.

- in CertAin CoUntrieS, women trAVeLinG At ALL – Let ALone BY themSeLVeS, with A ComPAnion who iS not their hUSBAND, or eVen with A femALe ComPAnion – iS frowneD UPon. for YoUr SAfetY AnD Smooth PASSAGe YoU ShoULD AVoiD eYe ContACt with Men or GroUPS of Men AnD CertAinLY YoU ShoULD not initiAte or hAVe ProLonGeD ConVerSAtionS with them. in Some CULtureS thiS MeAnS YoU Are AVAiLABLe AnD it CoULD CreAte A ProBLem YoU CertAinLY Don't neeD.

- toUtS – PeoPLe trYinG to SeLL YoU merChAnDiSe – Are A fACt of Life for ALL trAVeLerS. LeArn to PoLiteLY AnD firmLY SAY, 'no thAnK YoU' with A SmiLe if YoU CAn MUSter one, AnD SimPLY rePeAt it oVer AnD oVer. it MAY – wiLL – tAKe A whiLe BUt theY wiLL eVentUALLY Get the hint.

SMILE - YOU'RE ON YOUR WAY

Finally, all the dreaming, planning, organizing and running around has come to a glorious point and you are at long last 'traveling'. A couple of things to note:

Expectations about the whole traveling gig can, on occasion, get too high. It can certainly be fun and amazing but it's never consistently so. Sometimes it's tiring when the bus trip threatens never to end. Sometimes it's frustrating when you have had no problems with security throughout your entire journey and all of a sudden you're asked to unpack every last bit of underwear you possess without being told why. Sometimes it's frightening when you wonder if you will be run off the road by a wild truck that is dangerously overloaded. Sometimes you need every bit of your patience while you come to nearly wit's end waiting for some anonymous department bureaucrat to issue you a visa or ticket. Sometimes you experience every emotion in the book when you are caught in a bureaucratic tangle having lost your passport or baggage. **Delayed flights, bad weather, even natural disasters, can all become part of the experience when you travel.**

Many events or 'happenings' will test you when you're on the road; however, that is what you've chosen to do. There are always consequences of putting your hand up!

The best way to get through any rough patch when you're away is to simply try to bear it without completely falling apart or losing your composure. Think: I have all the time in the world. This [delay/problem/issue/annoyance/intrusion/theft/disaster] is happening for a reason – maybe it's for the best – and maybe I have something to learn or there is something else I still have to do here (or someone I still have to meet).

You can only ever be certain of one thing: you may never
know the real reason why 'stuff happens'.

REMEMBER:
THE ROAD IS THERE TO SHARE BUT THE CODE OF THE
ROAD IS UP TO EACH PERSON TO DIVINE FOR HERSELF.

"I HAD SO MANY AMAZING EXPERIENCES IN FIJI ... I WITNESSED SUNSETS THAT NO WORDS COULD DESCRIBE THE BEAUTY OF AND I TRAVELED TO A SMALL VILLAGE WHERE THE CHILDREN SANG & DANCED AROUND US VISITING FOREIGNERS. THEY LIVED BAREFOOT IN TINY SHACKS, WORE OLD CLOTHING, WALKED EVERYWHERE AND HAD VERY FEW MATERIAL POSSESSIONS. BUT THEY WERE ALWAYS SMILING & LAUGHING, ALWAYS OFFERING A HELPING HAND, TEACHING US SOME FIJIAN WORDS SHOWING US THE BEST SPOTS TO SNORKEL."

THESE BEAUTIFUL, FRIENDLY, WELCOMING PEOPLE HAD NEXT TO NOTHING AND YET WERE THE HAPPIEST PEOPLE I'VE EVER MET.

JESS MIGNONE
GIRLOSOPHER
MELBOURNE, AUSTRALIA

CHAPTER 6
ON THE ROAD

[THE ACT OF] TRAVELING IS OFTEN THE SAME AS TRAVELING BACK IN TIME – ESPECIALLY WHEN YOU TRAVEL TO LESSER DEVELOPED COUNTRIES THAN WHERE YOU ARE FROM. MY EXPERIENCE IN THE SOUTHWEST OF CHINA AND THE ISLANDS OF INDONESIA MADE THE HISTORY OF MY FAMILY AND MY COUNTRY COME TO LIFE.

This made me truly appreciate the achievements of our ancestors who built this life for us today.

NINA HAASE
GIRLOSOPHER
GERMANY

NINA HAASE
GIRLOSOPHER

PAGE # 171

CHAPTER # 6

CHAPTER
ON THE ROAD

BE OPEN, BE HONEST & JUST ... SMILE

"You've landed, navigated your trolley through the crowd, scooped up and stacked your bags like a pro, cut a swathe through security, immigration and customs with a smile and a confident nod, and now you're out in the terminal which is swarming like a beehive after something has disturbed it. You've officially arrived.

What now?

LEARN TO CHANGE AND ADAPT WHEN YOU'RE TRAVELING - MAKE FEAR YOUR FRIEND"

TIME-ZONE HASSLES

Change your watch as soon as you can to the time zone you are in. If your watch is digital and allows for multiple settings, switch to 24-hour time and plug in both your current local-time and your home-time zones. That way you will make the phone call at the right time (after 7:30 a.m. or 7:30 p.m.) so whoever you ring doesn't assume the worst when they receive a call at 3:00 a.m. when you meant to call at 3:00 p.m.!

GETTING GOING

THE GIRLO TRAVEL SURVIVAL KIT

TIME-ZONE HASSLES
GETTING GOING

175

ON THE ROAD

CHAPTER 6

If you are being met at the airport or train/bus terminal, try to stand still so whoever is meeting you can actually see you. If it is a hotel transfer bus driver, they will hold up a placard with your name(s) on it. Go with the porters to the van, which should have some sort of identifying logo of the hotel on it.

If you have no arrangement with anyone to collect you, then you should get a taxi to your accommodation. Go to the line. A taxi official will occasionally give you a ticket or voucher, which means they will allocate you a cab as one becomes available. The piece of paper they give you will often provide information about the correct cab fare from the airport/terminal to the city so you don't pay too much. Some countries have imposed a flat fee to prevent foreigners and tourists from being exploited by unscrupulous drivers.

If you are transferring to a domestic flight, catch the shuttle to the domestic terminal or, if it is possible and safe, walk to the domestic terminal to check-in there. Even if you have a fair bit of time between flights, it's better to go across; at least you'll be more likely to get a seat to relax in before you board again.

Try not to hang around looking 'clueless' at terminals of any description: you'll be a beacon for touts and fake cab drivers, other commission-based 'travel' or 'tour' guide-types who will try to sell you a tour or make you book into some hotel based on a promotion that requires you to go to a dreadful buffet. **The key is to be swift, brisk and efficient**. If you look as though you know what you're doing (even if you don't!) you're less likely to be a target.

CHECKING IN
AND TRAVEL WORK

Ensure you receive a non-smoking room as smoking rooms **always smell**, well, like an ashtray. Get two keys and keep them in separate spots in case you lose one. At the same time you should ask if there are any special events on either locally or generally. **Hotel receptionists and concierges usually know what's going on** and they're almost always very helpful and friendly. **Use them**!

Ask if there is an in-house grocery store and buy yourself a bottle of fresh water. Do check that the seal is not broken. Use this to **clean your teeth once you arrive** in your room – it's a quick fix to feeling faded and jaded after traveling. Unpack a couple of things, pull out your map and guide book stuff. Then have a **shower, put on some fresh clothes or simply lie down and put your feet up**. The first leg of the trip is done!

You should **have a small amount of the correct foreign currency so you can survive at least one day** without having to change money or go to a bank. I personally think that people carry on far too much about exchange rates – sometimes they end up quibbling over what amounts to be fifty cents. The main thing about money is this:

NEVER GO ANYWHERE SKETCHY
OR PUT YOURSELF IN A POSITION OF DANGER
OR COMPROMISE JUST TO GET A SO-CALLED
'BETTER RATE'.

You can always change money with traveler's checks or currency at a hotel if it's a decent one. They often have the same or better rates than the banks in some places. Most hotels charge a small fee/ commission but it's a whole lot better than being at risk in some Dodgy Brothers Inc. back street money-changing venue! If they don't change money, ask where the nearest bank is.

HOT GIRLO TIP

Always have small denominations of money on you. This is especially important if you are going to be out at night. There may not be a shop or place open where you can change a large bill or cash a traveler's check. Large bills tend to invite assumptions of wealth (even if it's the last of your money!) and this can cause headaches. Break large amounts down so you always have tip money handy or just smaller bills that local vendors and taxi drivers won't have trouble giving you change for. Be aware at all times of where you will be going and what you can expect to pay. And for goodness sake never get into a situation where you can't afford to settle an account or pay the bill!

RITUALS TO TRAVEL BY

Now that you are away, **putting some ritual into each new stage of your journey will make arrivals and departures at each place special for you**. Make a small shrine next to your bed in your room. You could do this by using a silk scarf or pashmina wrap, perhaps a small Buddha or crucifix, and some photos of your loved ones, maybe a flower and some crystals. **Say some positive words to the Universe — to the Travel Gods!** Thank them for all the wonderful opportunities and consciously invoke the feeling of gratitude that this is indeed possible for you.

You can take your spirituality with you everywhere. It helps you to tune into it and your guidance will only be enhanced. It's a bit like a meditation, or a little piece of home that you take with you. It will ground you and keep you centered so you will make good decisions and have powerful, positive experiences.

Arriving at your destination does bring with it a sense of relief and possibility. A shower! Clean clothes! Bed! Oh, what amazing concepts! A new room is symbolic. It's a fresh canvas (well, hopefully it is fresh!) to draw new memories from. A reminder: just because there is housekeeping or a maid (whom you may never see), this is no excuse to trash your accommodation. I'm frequently astonished when I visit someone in their hotel room or wherever it is that they are staying and find that it is covered from the door to the walls in clothes, books, shoes, plastic bags and ... there is stuff ... just ... everywhere.

A sound habit to get into is to keep the room orderly – and keep things systematic. You don't lose things, you don't invite theft and you won't feel like packing up to leave requires a super-human effort! Be respectful at all times in your temporary digs. Just because you pay to stay doesn't mean you get to make a crazy mess! Imagine the dreadful clean-up tasks which have befallen some poor housekeepers after people have checked out. Just because you don't see them doesn't mean they don't deserve your utmost consideration and respect. If anything they deserve it even more: after all, it's their hard work you're undoing!

E.T. PHONE HOME!

NOW WOULD BE A PERFECT TIME TO CALL HOME
(CHECK YOUR WATCH!)

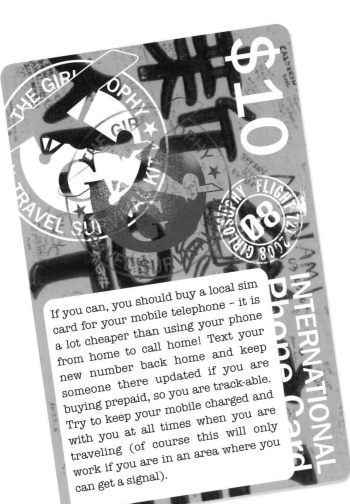

If you can, you should buy a local sim card for your mobile telephone – it is a lot cheaper than using your phone from home to call home! Text your new number back home and keep someone there updated if you are buying prepaid, so you are track-able. Try to keep your mobile charged and with you at all times when you are traveling (of course this will only work if you are in an area where you can get a signal).

PACE - DON'T RACE - YOURSELF

Whether you are in a large group, a family or with one other traveling companion, **it can be tricky hanging out 24-7.** Traveling with others can be brutal! **Not everyone has the same energy levels, nor the same level of desire** to see every single tourist icon in a destination. Some people just want to shop, others to walk the entire length of New York City on foot.

Run your own race! Just pace yourself and don't let anyone bully you into doing more than you feel you should – you'll get exhausted anyway, so it might as well be on your own terms!

There's no need to rush. **Take your time**. The place you are visiting is not going to disappear and you won't miss anything if you don't rush around! Chill out and get into a nice, relaxed pace so you don't have a fleeting memory of things flashing by.

SMELL THE ROSES (OR THE MARIGOLDS)
IN MOROCCO / PARIS / MADRID / DELHI...

GETTING YOUR BEARINGS

If you are the type of person who has an in-built compass in their brain and you always know where you are then you probably never get lost. For the rest of us, however, **sometimes getting our bearings is difficult**. When all the buildings in a place you have never been to before look the same or the lack of landmarks by which to orientate yourself becomes a problem, then it's time to narrow the focus.

Start locally with where you are staying. What major road is it on or near? Can you work out where the sun comes up or where it sets? If you find:

YOU'RE IN A STRANGE PLACE
YOU'RE LOST AT NIGHT
YOU'VE LOST YOUR SENSE OF DIRECTION
YOU'VE FORGOTTEN YOUR ADDRESS

you need to think clearly and slow down.

Don't rush off in any direction because you have panicked – **try to work out how far you have come and how long it took you to get there**. Check your map – perhaps you just need to find a street sign to figure it out. **If it is night time, be cautious and try to stay near bright lights, people and busy places**. Sit down at a café, buy a cup of tea and study the map calmly. Maybe the waiter can help you. It's better to ask someone who is attached to a place (i.e. working), as they will be more helpful and truthful. Hopefully you have your hotel or accommodation business card with you.

Whatever you do, don't panic. Try to find a phone and call the hotel. Maybe they can help you get back there, hand the phone to the waiter if you have to! Be intrepid and be brave, you're only lost, and it won't be for long.

CUSTOMS - NOT JUST AN AIRPORT THING!

Some of the customs of the local people may seem 'medieval' or a 'throwback to the dark ages' to many of us, however this is not home – it's not what you're used to! When you travel, you're the visitor and the guest, and **you must honor your host** while you are there, **no matter how strange or onerous it seems**. The customs of a culture or place are what make your trips full of extraordinary memories. For example:

- Sometimes you need to remove your shoes before you enter a house (Hawaii, Bali, Japan).
- Sometimes you are not supposed to turn your back on the Gods or the deities (Hindu religion, India).
- Sometimes it is protocol to kiss on both sides of the face when you meet someone, even for the first time (Argentina, Brazil and most of South America).
- Sometimes you are not meant to enter certain places if you have your period (sacred places all over the world).
- Sometimes you are meant to eat dates at the time when the Imam signals the fast is to be broken (Kashmir, Pakistan, parts of Africa and anywhere that celebrates Ramadan – Islamic countries).
- Sometimes you are meant to wear a certain type or style of garment to enter a temple or a scared site (Bali, Sri Lanka, the Middle East) or remove your shoes (everywhere in Asia), or cover your head (some churches in Italy).
- Sometimes you are going to offer and be offered in return a sacred scarf upon greetings or farewells (Tibet).

THERE ARE MILLIONS OF CUSTOMS! MAKE YOUR JOURNEY BOTH SACRED AND MEMORABLE BY PARTICIPATING WILLINGLY AND WITH ENTHUSIASM. IT'S WHY YOU'RE THERE.

"WE STARTED OUR TRIP IN AMSTERDAM AND WE DROVE THROUGH THE MIDDLE EAST IN A CAMPER VAN, JUST THE TWO OF US. BECAUSE WE WERE TWO EUROPEAN GIRLS WITH BLONDE HAIR AND BLUE EYES WE GOT A POLICE ESCORT THROUGH PAKISTAN! AFTER THAT WE ALWAYS COVERED UP COMPLETELY EVEN THOUGH THE TEMPERATURES WERE EXTREMELY HOT.

BUT WHEN WE WERE IN IRAN
SOMETIMES BEING COVERED UP
GOT SO UNCOMFORTABLE
WE WOULD PULL OVER
TO THE SIDE OF THE ROAD,
LOWER THE BLINDS
DOWN ON ALL THE WINDOWS AND
HOP IN THE BACK
SO WE COULD TAKE OFF THE
HEAD GEAR AND
THE LONG DRESSES AND SIT IN OUR
NORMAL CLOTHES JUST FOR A MINUTE TO
COOL OFF.
BUT ONE TIME WE DID THIS IN A
REMOTE VILLAGE,
A CROWD HAD
GATHERED AROUND THE VAN AND THEY HAD
THEIR FACES PRESSED TO THE
WINDOWS AND WITH A SHOCK
WE REALIZED THAT THEY WERE ALL STARING
IN THROUGH THE
CRACKS
AT US
IN OUR
SHORTS
&
T-SHIRTS!

ULRICHA & EVA
INTREPID GIRLO TRAVELERS
HOLLAND

BLENDING IN WITH THE LOCALS

Apart from anything, **following protocol or custom allows you to pass relatively unnoticed**. Blending in means you won't be the focus of unwanted interactions from those whom you may have offended – or even intrigued – by your actions, however unknowingly. **Primarily it's about being respectful**. There is no point in angering or offending people. And no one wants to cause a scene.

The golden rule:

IF YOU DON'T THINK YOU CAN HANDLE THE CUSTOMS OR RELIGIOUS PRACTICES OF A PARTICULAR COUNTRY, THEN IT IS ONE THAT SHOULD NOT BE ON YOUR LIST.

MODESTY IS A HIDDEN QUALITY (FLESH IS NOT BEST)

There are some countries and cultures where the custom of covering up exposed skin is essential. This is non-negotiable – if they do not allow you to go topless on the beach, please don't. It might be OK to do it on Bondi Beach in Australia or Biarritz in France, but it's not OK in the Hamptons in the US (where you can be arrested for indecent exposure) and certainly not on the beach in Bali, Indonesia where you will upset people greatly. Likewise, don't wear thigh-revealing shorts if you are visiting a country where women are wearing burqhas or hijabs. Common sense please! Cover your hair and head and wear long sleeves. Wear a long-sleeved loose fitting tunic over long pants for comfort and cover. Please, don't wear revealing, tight or super-clingy T-shirts, nor strapless tops or tops where your bra straps are showing, nor should you wear tank tops or singlets where your shoulders and bare arms are revealed, nor super 'low-rider' jeans. Flesh is not best. In some places (read: most of India, the Middle East, Eastern Europe, parts of Africa) that is considered to be pornography and you will offend the locals. **Please don't!**

TIPS 'R' ALL OF US

I mentioned a tipping strategy before but **you need to decide how you will tip someone before it becomes embarrassing**. Even if you are traveling on the proverbial shoestring – in some places it is mandatory. **You need to tip, so you may as well get used to it**. The old excuse, 'But they are getting paid to do their job', isn't correct in the way we know it at home.

Some people earn almost nothing from the establishment and rely on tips for their pay. And you will be letting people down if you don't do it. New York cabbies have been known to get out and abuse people on the footpath if they don't give a reasonable tip.

Find out what is customary in the place you are visiting. **If you do the right thing, the right thing will be done to you**.

WHAT COMES AROUND GOES AROUND, TRULY.

MEETING PEOPLE

There's no doubt that meeting people is one of the highlights of traveling. It's the joy of connection that makes the travel experience rich and why it's worth getting off the couch to go abroad. Being a traveler means you are open to receiving others and hearing their stories.

It's about sharing who you are and swapping notes about life and love, although you may even come from completely different worlds.

Talk and listen to those whom you meet on the road. It may only be in passing and you may only share a minute or three, but **the wisdom that passes through each of you may be the real pearl ... and last you a lifetime.**

LOST IN TRANSLATION

It is both polite and incredibly useful to have at least a few key phrases on hand when you travel. Even if you don't feel confident in your language skills, you can still smile and try a 'Hello' or 'Good Morning' or 'Thank you' in the local language. **It's so important to at least try to communicate as it helps to break down the barriers of foreign-ness.**

Others will smile back at you and you'd be amazed at what the combination of your efforts, their willingness and your smile can achieve. **You are an ambassador for your country and your gender, so have a go!**

Some key phrases to learn ahead of arrival -
(call it your homework!):

- heLLo
- PLeASe
- thAnK YoU
- GooD MorninG
- GooD niGht
- MY nAMe iS ...
- whAt iS YoUr nAMe PLeASe?
- how MUCh DoeS thiS CoSt?
- CAn YoU PLeASe heLP Me with ... ?
- CAn YoU PLeASe teLL Me
  where ... Street iS?

And then there is also:

- i LoVe YoU

A GOLDEN RULE:
THIS LAST ONE SHOULD PROBABLY NOT
BE OVER-USED WHEN YOU TRAVEL!

I LOVE YOU
THE LANGUAGE OF LOVE

TE QUIERO .... SPANISH

JE T'AIME .... FRENCH

ICH LIEBE DICH .... GERMAN

TI' AMO .... ITALIAN

IK HOU VAN JOU .... DUTCH

AMO-TE .... PORTUGUESE

JEG ELSKER DEG ..... NORWEGIAN

FOREIGN AFFAIRS

Ah yes, the look of love is in their eyes but what on earth are they truly saying? **Love on the road less traveled is certainly a rollercoaster ride**. Many people meet who they believe is their soulmate while traveling. Anything is possible, but there are heartbreaking stories aplenty so when you bat your eyes at the cabana guy, know there will be consequences!

It almost shouldn't need to be said but of course any sexual interaction you engage in should **absolutely adhere to safe sex practices**. Safe sex is a practice that is international and mandatory these days.

HIV/AIDS AND HEPATITIS C DO NOT RECOGNIZE NATIONALITY OR BORDERS.

No matter what your preference or beliefs, you should be especially careful when you travel if you plan on becoming intimately involved with someone. **For goodness sake, use condoms!** And you should both have a blood test if you plan not to, to protect each other. Of course the only truly safe sex is no sex and you may consider abstinence as a lifestyle choice to be completely sure.

Relationships when you are traveling invariably have a more intense angle to them than normal. Language and cultural differences aside, often there is a completely different mindset to comprehend as well. So while this can be enthralling, it can also blind you to the reality of the situation. Be open to the moment, enjoy meeting and interacting with people – you might indeed meet your soulmate – however try to be conscious that reality can also be a somewhat confronting wake-up call.

FOOD STUFF -
WHAT TO EAT AND WHAT NOT TO EAT

I wrote about this at some length in **Girlosophy - Real Girls Eat**, however, being healthy and staying that way really comes down to a couple of things when you're on the road:

- WASHING YOUR HANDS A LOT
  (AND BEFORE EACH MEAL OR ANY SNACK AT ALL).
- CHOOSING WHERE TO EAT WISELY.
- KNOWING WHAT NOT TO EAT.

When you're traveling, eating can be a gamble as you can't always check the hygiene of each establishment. As a rough rule of thumb I check the cleanliness of the interior and make a general decision based on the 'Feel' of the place. I also check how busy it is as this will have a bearing on food turnover, giving me some indication of the freshness of the food.

I **never choose salads** unless I am in the restaurant or café of a top hotel (these will always have high standards as they charge so much). **I peel fruit, eating only things like bananas, papayas, pineapples or oranges**, which need peeling. **Super hot or fried things are best** as any nasty bacteria that may be present are mostly killed in the cooking process. I **avoid dairy, poultry, eggs and certainly all meat** if I am in hot climates. So that leaves rice, rice ... and rice! Oh ... and couscous, legumes, vegetables and noodle dishes, curries and dumplings and hot soups, etc. **Basically if it's fresh veg, boiled, fried or super hot, and it's not meat or dairy, you should be fine.**

DRINKING THE WATER

Drinking water that is not pure is one way to seriously derail your trip. All drinking water should be bottled, sealed and fresh. Don't drink 'old' bottled water that's been rolling around the floor of the bus or van for a day or two, even if it's yours. Bacteria multiply quickly and that can be dangerous to your health.

Take a bottle of water with you when you leave on your day's sightseeing and drink frequently and regularly. **Buy fresh bottles as often as possible** – only refill a small (portable) bottle from a big one a few times before you replace the bottle entirely.

NEVER DRINK FROM THE TAP AND
DO NOT DRINK UNFILTERED WATER!

If you are trekking, water should always be fully boiled, and have purification tablets and/or iodine. Your guide should be able to explain how to boil and drink the water safely.

Note: When I travel I always clean my teeth using bottled water and the one time I forgot, I ended up with a very upset stomach and ruined birthday plans.

BE RIGOROUS AND BEWARE!

198.

DRINK SPIKING IS AN INTERNATIONAL CRIME

Never EVER let anyone you don't know or whom you may have only just met buy you a drink of any description. Even if they are offering you 'just a Coke' or any other form of soft drink, a polite and firm 'NO, THANK YOU' is the only answer. This is a golden rule of travel – no exceptions. You should only buy drinks from places where you can take the top off the bottle and break the seal yourself (or the bar tender should break it in your presence). **This is both a HEALTH and a SAFETY issue!**

WHEN YOUR STOMACH JUST CAN'T TAKE IT

Being ill when you're away is tough. It happens to all travelers at some point in their journey. **The key is to be onto it as soon as you can to manage the illness as best you can**. The major problem with all stomach problems, including diarrhea and vomiting, is that you're at risk of dehydration.

Read the literature on such illnesses and how to treat them. One of my mainstay remedies if I'm feeling a little 'off' is a rather unorthodox mix of dry toast, sliced banana pieces and Coca-cola. That and the relevant medication and lots of fresh water has had me back to form in no time.

If the illness continues and worsens – don't delay. Call the house or hotel doctor and/or get medical advice as soon as possible. It may be serious. **Please don't take unnecessary risks with your health. It's simply not worth it**.

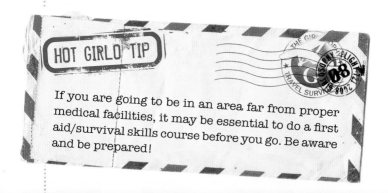

HOT GIRLO TIP

If you are going to be in an area far from proper medical facilities, it may be essential to do a first aid/survival skills course before you go. Be aware and be prepared!

TRAVEL MATES BLUES

Arguments on the road are a fact of life. One person wants to go one way and the other swears the map is wrong or stupid and wants to go home. **This is where all traveling mates may need to recall the concept of 'team work'.**

It is unrealistic to expect everyone to agree all the time, especially when there are about a million small and not so small decisions that are being made on the hop on a daily basis. **Having an agreed-upon strategy to deal with issues or dilemmas will help.**

CALL IT OUT
CALL IT OFF
CALL A TRUCE

You simply can't 'argue' your way around the planet. Well, you can but you'd be missing the point entirely! So if it gets to the situation where you are not doing anything except arguing, something's got to change. And it's probably both of you!

The old saying is that if you can travel with someone you should marry them. Well, it's the same with friendship – you'll either be friends for a city or friends for life when you travel with someone. So if you argue, agree to disagree, call it off (the argument, that is!) and call a truce. **Figure out how you can both be happy – put all options on the table and work out who gets to choose this time, on the condition that the other person gets to choose the next time.** It's mature to share.

UH-OH!
WHEN THINGS GO PEAR-SHAPED

If things are not going according to plan and you are truly having a bad time on your travels then it's time to reassess the situation. Being away and enduring hardship is harder in another country where the support network you have at home doesn't exist. It might be time to pack up and return home to regroup and return with renewed energy (and bank account!), or ... it might be time to stay put and lick your wounds if that is the case.

One of the less known things about traveling is that **you tend to attract the same level of experiences as you put out with your energy**. So, if you're in a downwards spiral, all sorts of negative stuff starts to happen. Things can seem to go from bad to worse in a heartbeat! If you went traveling to avoid problems or issues you were having at home, then very likely they didn't stay at the departure lounge. **You can't just leave things behind because you got on a plane**! They most likely came with you.

If you were having money problems at home then probably you'll have them when you travel too. If you were hanging out with a bad scene or you hooked up with the wrong crowd at home, the chances are the same will happen when you're away.

But **the beauty about life is that you can rewrite the script anytime you want**. If you resolve to get to the bottom of the issues – and take personal responsibility for your part – all sorts of new things will start flowing your way.

"TRAVELING IS ALL ABOUT GETTING AN ACT (AND KEEPING IT TOGETHER)"

Traveling can be as spiritual or as material as you are. **It's all about your orientation (positive? negative?) and your perception of how things work**. If you truly want to change your life in a fresh context you will have to realize that who you are is already in place but that refinements and changes to that 'Self' are always possible.

THE ROAD IS A GREAT PLACE –
PROBABLY THE IDEAL PLACE –
TO WORK THIS STUFF OUT.

CRISIS AT HOME?

Keeping in touch with home is great but occasionally the news is not so good. Grandma is in hospital or Dad has had an accident or maybe one of your good friends has lost a sibling or parent tragically. **How you cope and what you do with this news is very much up to you**.

You're a long way from home and there may be only so much you can do. If you decide to return to 'be there' and feel it is the most appropriate thing to do, then start making arrangements. Otherwise, perhaps you should phone or email daily to get updates. Ask your parents if they need your support. **Talk things through – all the pros and cons of staying versus coming back**. They may not want you to come back just for them or even just for you.

If you're going to be grieving or not at your best for the foreseeable future, then you may have to consider the feelings of your travel companions too. No one else, can make the decision for you. However, you need to accept that it can seem excruciatingly hard to make the choice.

It is worth remembering that the Earth will still be here, but your grandmother won't always be. **Whatever you decide to do – stay or go home – that's okay. The decision is entirely yours**.

TROUBLE IS WITHOUT BORDERS

Trouble comes in all forms and definitely doesn't recognize borders! It can happen anywhere. If you find yourself or your traveling companion(s) in trouble when you are traveling, act calmly, decisively and quickly. If you do not speak the language of your host country, you should try to get them to understand that you need an interpreter.

Here are a few situations and possible solutions. But the most important thing to remember **in all situations is to act sensibly**. You don't want to make the situation worse with rash or emotional decisions.

PROBLEMS WITH AUTHORITIES

If your issue involves police, security or customs, as much as possible you should cooperate fully with their requests. **Don't make things worse by arguing with them**, getting angry or causing a scene. Be aware that they are usually just doing their job, so **being pleasant and polite** – even if (especially if!) it turns out that you are in the wrong – your manners and politeness **will only be to your advantage long-term**.

Do stay cool and calm. Breaking down into a sobbing mess will not necessarily help your situation. You need to be aware and not get into the emotional side of whatever is happening as it may cloud your judgment when you most need it.

If you feel uneasy – that is, you get a sense that whoever is detaining you or dealing with you is or are not trustworthy or if you just get a bad vibe about the way things are going – **insist on being allowed to make a telephone call to the embassy or the local consulate authority**. If it looks serious or if you or your companion(s) are going to be held or detained or required to do something to be released, ask if you can call your/their parents or anyone local who may be able to help you.

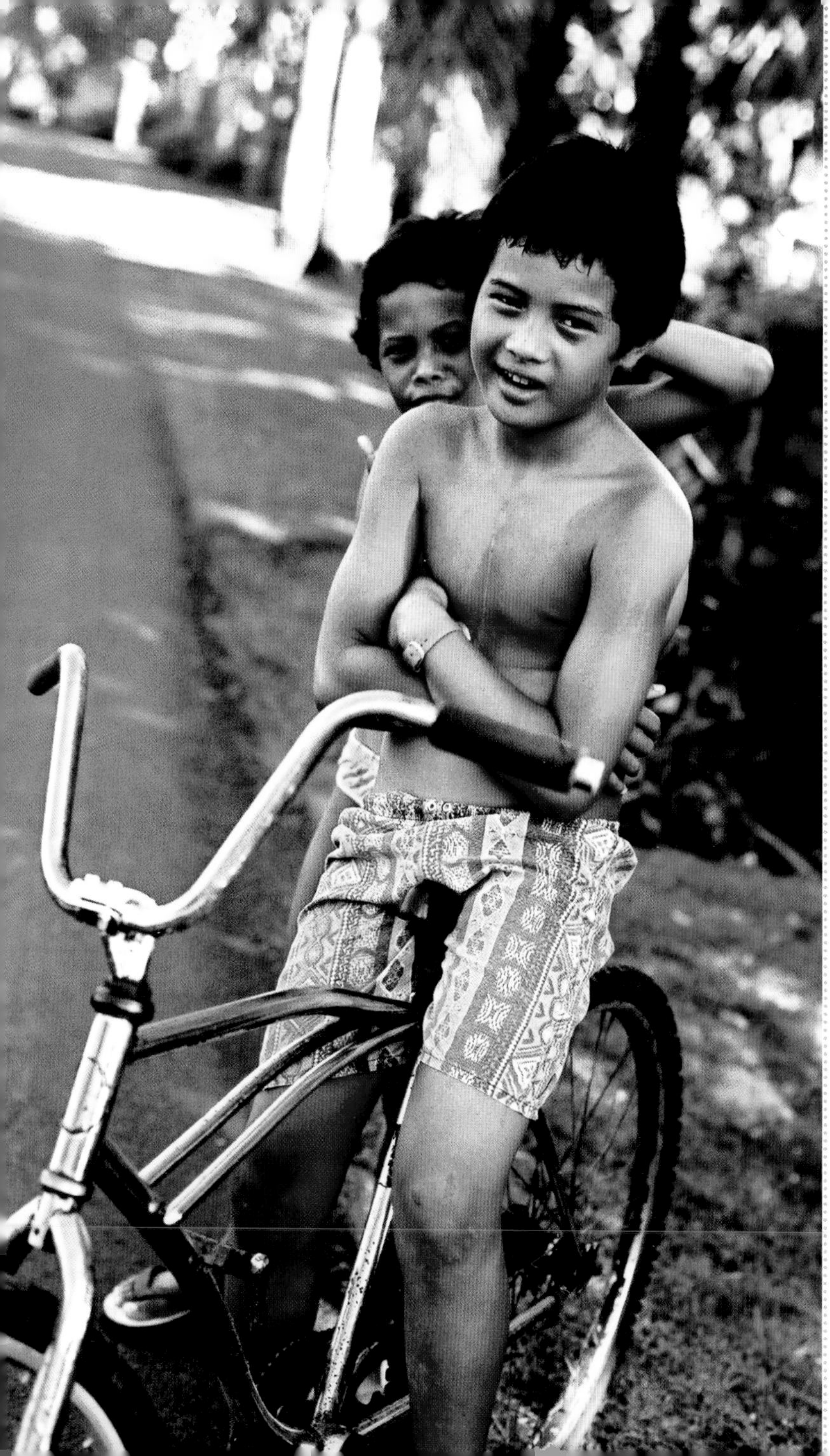

LEGAL HASSLES

If legal issues arise insist on your rights for legal representation immediately. Do not say or sign anything without having legal represen-tation. If it involves your travel companion(s) then try to arrange for them to have a lawyer present and call the local embassy on their behalf. **Above all, do not make any statements or written confessions or admissions without a lawyer present to witness how the statement was obtained.**

If you have broken the law, **you should be aware that you are very much in the hands of the lawmakers and the judicial system of that country.** This also means that often there is little your own country can do for you except to ensure at official levels that you are being treated correctly and fairly under international obligations. But as the newspapers so often reveal, this is not always the case and you certainly can't rely on it.

MEDICAL EMERGENCIES

If the problem involves a medical emergency or an accident, **you'll have to be quick thinking to ensure your own or your companion's safety and the appropriate medical care.** These things can only be dealt with at the time and if this happens you may be under immense pressure to manage the situation.

Your resuscitation skills and basic first aid knowledge are useful until you can get to a hospital or a doctor. Call or ask someone to call for medical help and get the clear understanding from them that they have done this. Double-check and check again! **If you can't speak the language, call the embassy if possible to explain your predicament** and get assistance locally, even if it's just someone on the phone who can act as a go-between.

HELP IS AT HAND

Always keep a few key phone numbers handy in your purse or wallet if you are going out at night or leaving your hotel for the day. If you have one, take your mobile out with you although check that you can get a signal with it wherever you go. **That way if something goes down** and you need to let someone know or contact the hotel or your friends whom you are staying with, **you'll have the jump on things**.

When you go into a crowded place, say a market or bazaar or at night in a night club, you should have a game plan to **check in with each other at regular intervals** or (preferably) arrange to hang out together as much as possible. Have a plan to regroup at a specific place if you do become separated. **Work out clearly and precisely in advance how you can meet up again in any situation**.

The 'Buddy System' is a **good deterrent** to people who don't have your interests at heart (and, sadly these types are everywhere). Those who are truly up to no good feel less confident to try to take advantage of you if you are clearly with someone or socializing together in a tight group.

If you or your companion become lost or separated from each other, stay calm, think clearly and try not to draw unnecessary attention to your predicament. Search the logical places first (the toilets, the main entrance where you came in through, the nearest restaurant or drinks vendor), then return again to the last place where you saw each other. Try not to move away too far when you are looking or searching as mostly people do come back to the same spot!

209

If you are the victim of a crime, you should report it to the local authorities. If it is a serious crime – you have been assaulted or suffered any injuries, etc., – you should get a full medical report and clearance before continuing on your trip.

If the crime involves personal loss, such as stolen items, then you will need to obtain a certified copy of the police report to bring home with you in order to make a claim on travel insurance. Be aware that if you are unable to prove the theft or loss occurred, insurance companies will almost certainly not pay you compensation.

HOT GIRLO TIP

Always keep your consulate or embassy hotline in your purse or wallet (or better yet tucked into a pocket of your jeans or skirt) when you go out. In addition, take the hotel notepad or the hostel business card with you with the phone numbers and contact details. This way, as a last option, even if you can't speak the language you can show it to a cab or bus driver and they can work out where you need to go.

HOT GIRLO TIP

Don't take your passport with you when you go out at night. If there is a safe in the hotel, leave it there or if there is no safe, lock it into your main bag. Take your driver's licence with one credit card and a small amount of cash or just a photo ID card with you instead. If you don't take everything with you, you can't lose everything at once!

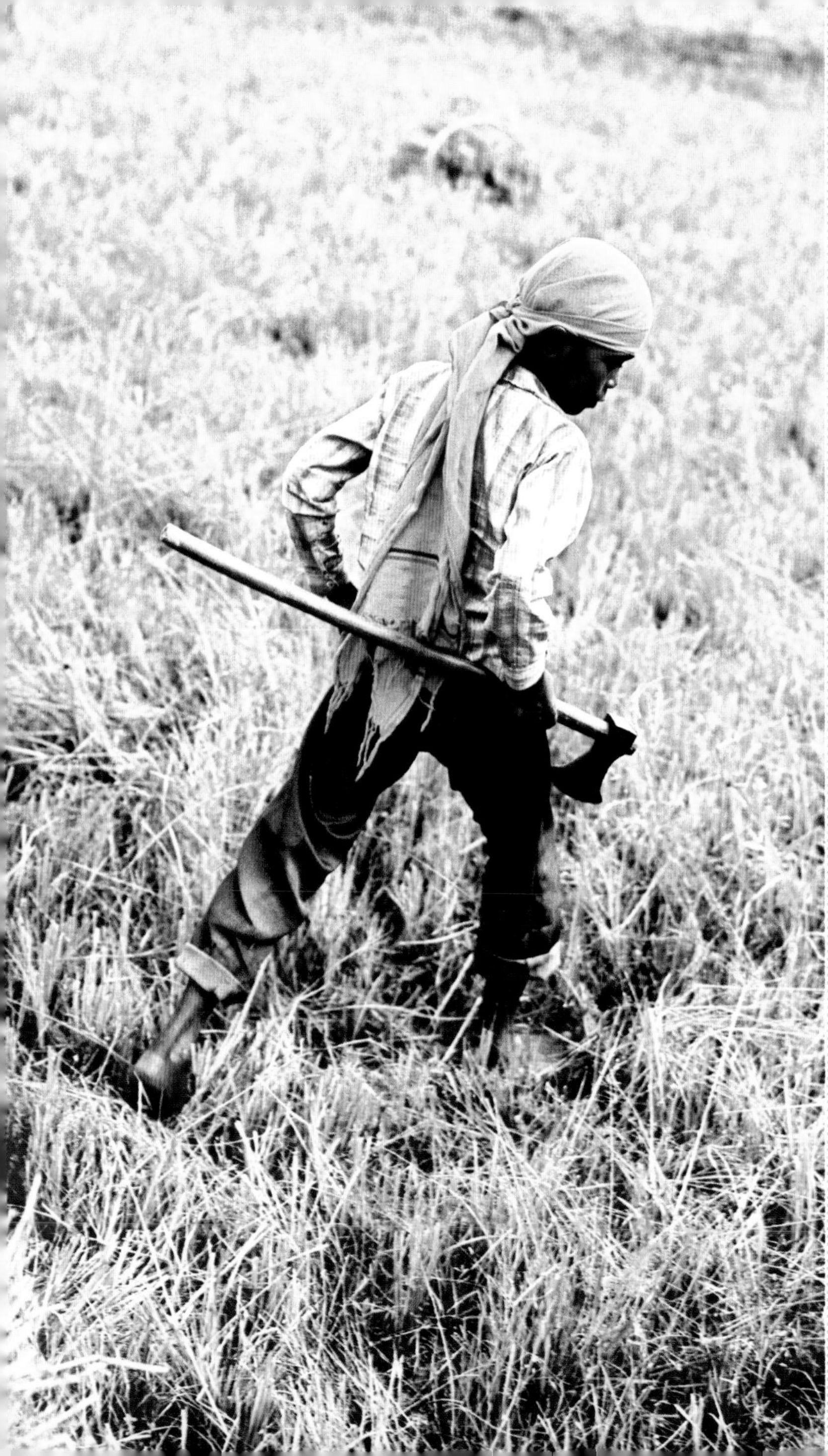

IT'S NOT EASY BEING GREEN

Travelers can be very hard on the environment. Despite the latest trend of eco-traveling, the cost of all the experiences, new-found knowledge and friendships is paid for by the Earth. **From the moment we leave our homes we impact the areas we move through**. Unfortunately this is not always in a positive way.

Starting with the fuel consumed by planes and buses, to the paper documents, ticketing, plastics and disposable items and the rubbish we leave behind, we need to be conscious of the actual and real cost of our travels. In some developing countries 'environmentally friendly' is a concept that has barely been heard of, so when we visit, we are having even more than an impact on the environment than we do at home. You'll probably even be shocked to see the extent of pollution in some countries. That is why **we need to be ultra-conscious while we are out in the world**:

- BECOME AN ECO-TRAVELER and try as far as possible to make your journey carbon-neutral – recycle, dispose of all things properly.
- RECYCLE YOUR TOWELS when the hotel offers this as an option.
- DON'T USE A BUNCH OF THOSE DISPOSABLE PLASTIC DRINKING CUPS on the plane – keep one and reuse it for the whole journey.
- FILL UP AND DRINK OUT OF YOUR WATER BOTTLE instead of buying soft drinks that are mostly not recycled (clean your bottle regularly).
- INVESTIGATE CARBON TRADING before you leave and make being a green traveler part of your trip plan. Then you can truly say your journey is not literally costing the Earth!

213

LEAVE
ONLY
FOOTPRINTS,
TAKE
ONLY
PICTURES.

WILDERNESS SAYING

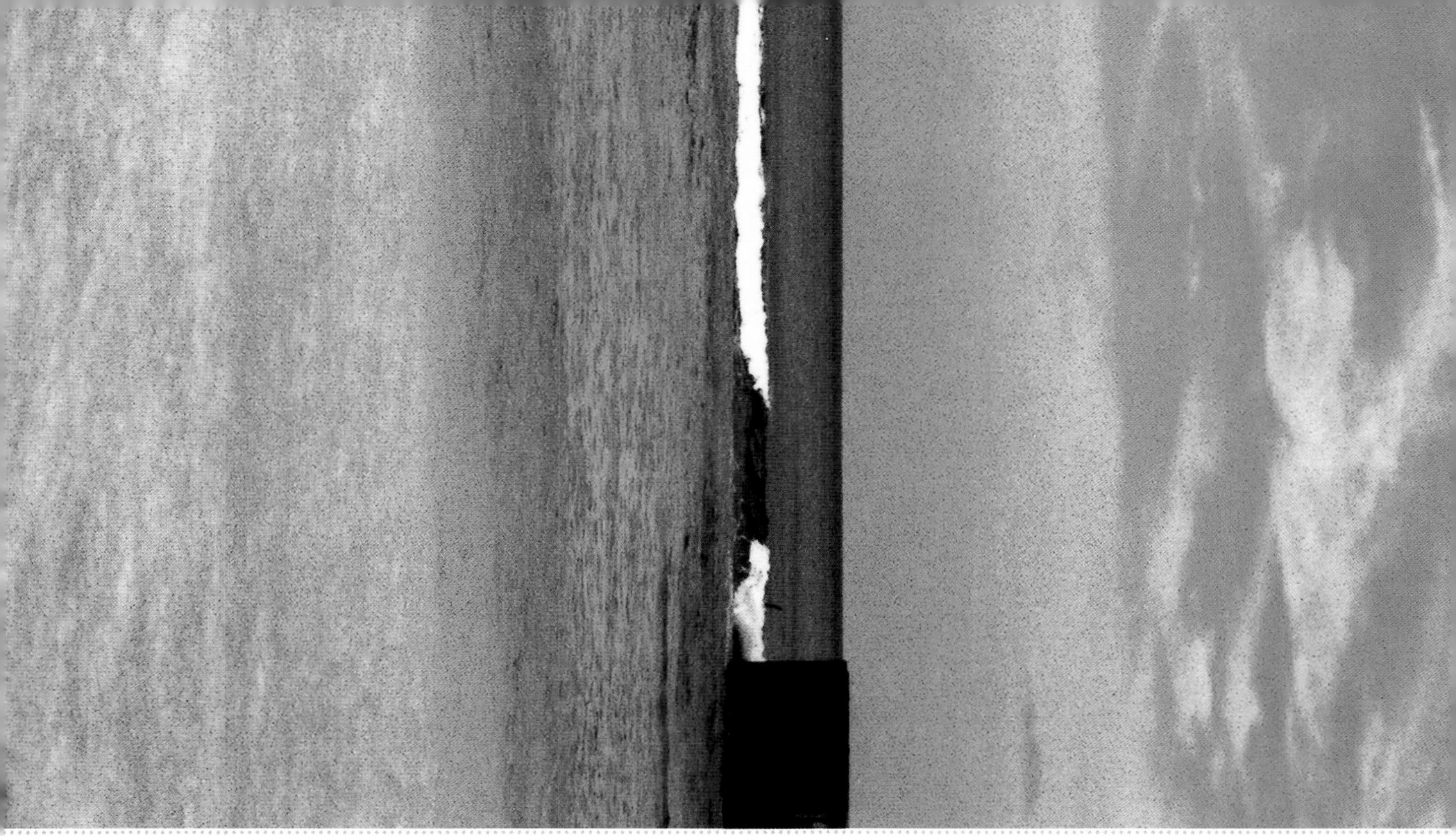

MEMORIES

One of the best parts of traveling is the visual stimulation of being in a completely new place. Taking photographs is so much fun in such an environment. No matter whether you shoot film or digital, do try to be discreet.

Don't shove your camera lens in the face of someone who is praying or worshiping or even having a private moment. Get a clear sign that they don't mind their photo being taken, or if you cannot obtain their permission, even if you decide to take the shot, make it a wider shot so they would not necessarily know you were focused on them. **Remember, there are many ways of using a camera, but it's sometimes better to miss the shot than offend someone. I have missed a million photographs but I still carry them with me – on the walls of my mind.**

✗ ALSO, PLEASE DON'T:

- Ham it up for the camera with inappropriate poses and positions in front of sacred places or monuments - be respectful and mindful at all times.
- Take photographs if it says 'NO PHOTOGRAPHS'.
- Take photographs of people worshiping or praying unless you have their permission beforehand.
- Take photographs if people want to be paid for it, unless they are 'dressed up for tourist photographs' and then you must pay them.
- Photograph every single iconic tourist destination you visit - buy the postcard instead, as the images are often taken by professionals who need to make a living and the pictures could quite possibly be better, particularly if the light's bad on the day!

GUArD, JoDhPUr PALACe, rAJhASthAn, inDiA

If a picture is worth a thousand words, the reverse is also true. Write down in lucid prose your impressions and feelings about a place. Your journal can become your sketch book - who says a drawing plus a paragraph or a few lines isn't as good as a photograph?

Be inspired with your journal and travel writing!

Real Girl and long-time girlosopher, Sam Symonds, creates exquisite hand-painted travel journals that are both beautiful and inspirational. (See her work in **My Girlosophy: How to write your own life**).

GETTING MEMENTOS HOME INTACT

Make your gifts small and special. There is no sense buying the most enormous, heavy book or object and then trying to get it home. It makes sense to ship things if they are large or, better still, simply to buy small objects that will serve the purpose of being a lovely memento – and fit into your bag without tipping the scales at the check-in!

Look for small icons or little handmade statues or objects made from solid materials such as brass or wood, slim paperback books, cards, pens, small photo-sized artworks, handmade beaded or local jewelry, scarves, cushion covers, T-shirts, snow domes, small purses and handmade bags, textiles or sarongs. **Remember, some items, such as wooden objects, might need to be declared to customs**, and others, such as artefacts from national sites, are totally banned from leaving the country of origin! Ensure you know the rules and obey them.

Buying local handicrafts is a great way to support local businesses and it shows you care as well. Bargaining vendors down to ridiculously (unfairly) low levels, however, is not in the spirit of being a good traveler. Add another couple of dollars and make everyone happy!

Bubble-wrap all fragile and more breakable items to prevent damage and therefore disappointment on arrival. Securely roll them in the sweaters or jackets and then pack carefully in your bag. **Secure all items so they don't move around the bag**.

NO MATTER HOW SMALL,
A GIFT SAYS YOU WERE THINKING ABOUT THEM.

THE GIRLD TRAVEL SURVIVAL KIT

CHAPTER 7
COMING HOME

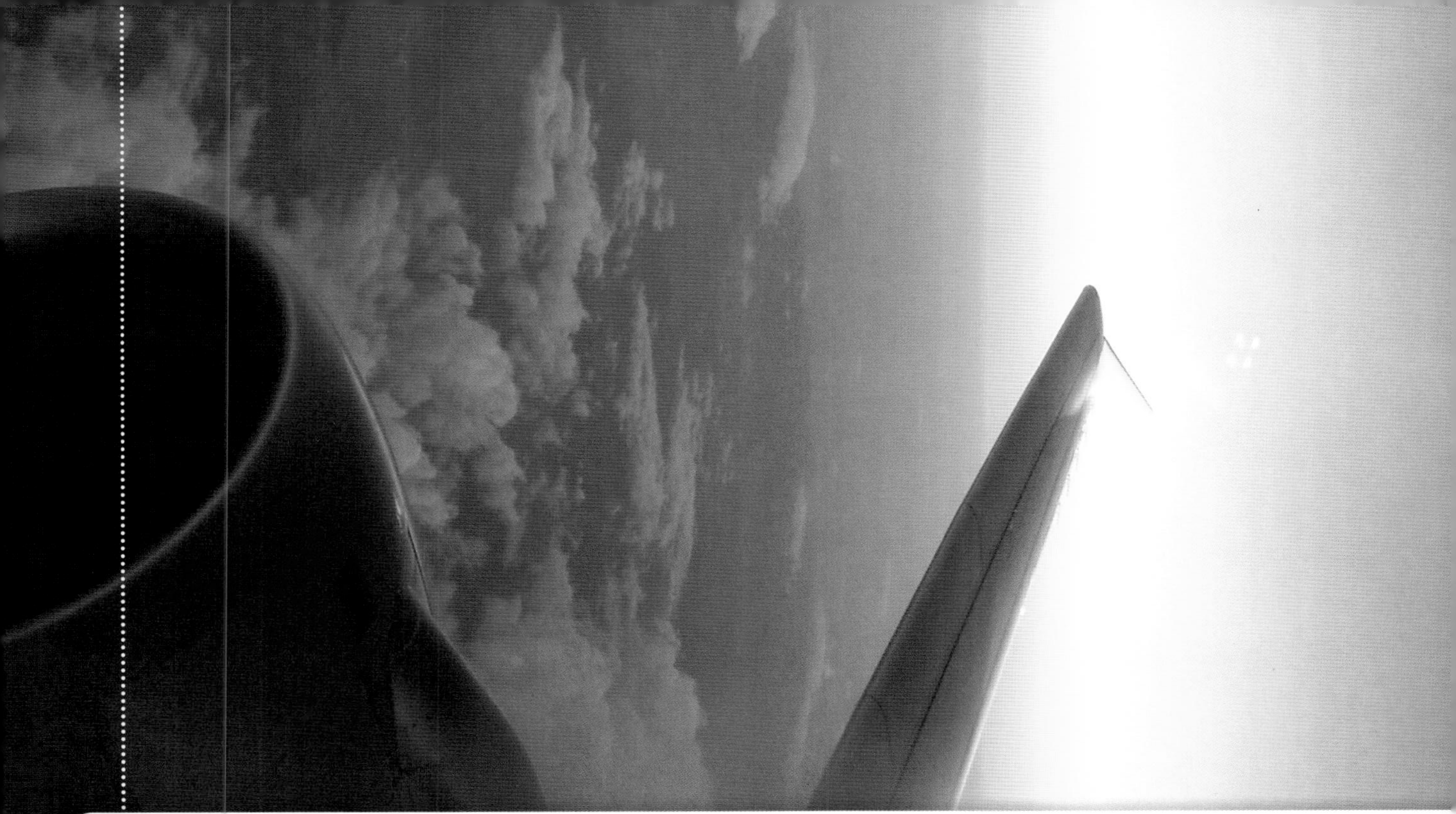

"
PLEASE LEAVE YOUR SEATBELTS
ON UNTIL THE CAPTAIN TURNS THE SEATBELT SIGN
OFF. PLEASE TAKE CARE WHEN OPENING OVERHEAD LOCKERS, THINGS MAY HAVE SHIFTED DURING THE FLIGHT. WE DO HOPE YOU ENJOYED FLYING WITH US TODAY AND IF YOU ARE TRAVELING ONWARDS THAT YOU HAVE A SAFE JOURNEY.

WE HOPE TO SEE YOU BACK WITH US IN THE

FRIENDLY SKIES SOON ...

"

You 'de-plane', head towards immigration to have your passport checked while your bags make their way off the luggage carousel for the final time. Soon **you're wheeling your trolley towards customs**. You pick up your board bags or snowboard bag at the special baggage doors – (it arrived! In one piece!) – And then **you line up, bleary-eyed, for the security X-ray**, also for the final time.

YOU ARE HOME.

Behind the wall and down the ramp are probably family members, your friends or your boyfriend. **There will be screams of delight, hugs, hands ruffling (new) hairdos, admiring smiles, stares, comments and pronouncements**. So that's it. You're back where it all began. How can it be so soon? Where did all that time go? It's hard to take in, but your dream trip has ended, for now

THE SHOCK OF THE NEW (AND THE OLD!)

Many travelers have a huge shock when they return home. Not because things are different, mostly it's due to the fact that you feel different. Even if you think you don't look different, you probably do. But more than appearances it's the perception that nothing seems the same, yet it is all the same! But you may look at your old bedroom and not see it in quite the same way.

And maybe no one else has noticed the change in you or, if they do, they are treating you as if you're just back and you're still you and life goes on. But you're not you. Well, you're not the 'old you'. **You're the 'new you'. The 'traveler you'.**

Others (family or friends) may also have changed in your absence, and as you notice these, you also notice that you don't get their changes! It's all a bit strange and weird. Your baby brother is old enough to be out with his mates at all times, mom or dad may have new hobbies which take up a lot of time and they're all busy, busy, busy. Maybe your home was renovated while you were away and your bedroom is half the size because your parents figured you'd be moving out when you came home. Your Bestie may have moved in with her boyfriend and started a new job. **Life moves on.**

But these changes are nothing compared to the shock of realizing how everything is still pretty much the same now that you're home. **You have had the journey and the experiences of a lifetime but now you're back to, well, the same old, same old.**

<u>SO WHAT HAPPENS NOW?</u>

" NO ONE REALIZES HOW BEAUTIFUL IT IS TO TRAVEL UNTIL [S]HE COMES HOME AND RESTS [HER] HEAD ON [HER] OLD, FAMILIAR PILLOW. " LIN YUTANG

MANAGING THE RE-ENTRY

Here is an arrival routine which may help you to settle in again – it works for me:

• RESET YOUR WATCH AND MOBILE PHONE – adjust to the new time zone. It helps to adjust mentally and minimizes jetlag (if only psychologically).

• CALL OR SMS WHOEVER IS MEETING YOU AT THE AIRPORT AS A COURTESY TO LET THEM KNOW THE PLANE HAS LANDED. It can be chaotic at the arrival terminals and this can be stressful for those waiting as they usually don't know what's happening, especially if the flight is delayed. Although, be aware, that in many airports the use of mobile phones in both immigration and through the clearance from customs is not allowed. But sometimes you will have a long walk between disembarkation and customs and if this is the case I typically do this then by switching my phone to silence. Please check signs first as you've come a long way on your travels and you will want to avoid any problems right at the end. Better to finish up on a good note!

• ONCE HOME, A CUP OF TEA, LIGHT SNACK AND A BIG GLASS OF WATER OR FRESH JUICE PLUS VITAMINS, including or especially echinacea, a multivitamin, and powdered vitamin C, to 'kill' any bugs that may have picked you up on the flight will be just the thing.

• UNPACK BAGS AND STORE BAGGAGE IMMEDIATELY.

• SORT WASHING AND PUT AWAY ANY CLEAN CLOTHES.

• PUT THE FIRST LOAD OF WASHING ON!

• PILE GIFTS, MEMENTOS AND PAPERWORK ON YOUR DESK for wrapping or filing, storing, etc.

• SHOWER, WASH AND DRY HAIR, AND GET INTO FRESH, COMFORTABLE CLOTHES. AHHH!

• TRY TO GET SOME SUN (it resets the body clock) by going for a brisk walk. A WALK IS ALSO RECOMMENDED BY HEALTH PROFESSIONALS AS IT GETS YOUR CIRCULATION MOVING AGAIN AFTER THE LONG FLIGHT AND PREVENTS DVT (deep vein thrombosis).

• SLEEP OR ... DEPENDING ON WHAT TIME YOU HAVE ARRIVED, STAY UP until a reasonable time to try and have a normal night's sleep.

• DRINK WATER, WATER, WATER.

• MAKE SOME LISTS OF THINGS-TO-DO THE FOLLOWING DAY.

HOMECOMING QUEEN

You may feel great. Your new-found confidence is a beacon to all and sundry. Since your arrival back home, your mobile is ringing off the hook, emails are flowing in from all corners of the globe, and you have so many new admirers that you have lost count. Because you are shining with the glow of someone who is alive and in the flow, you attract the 'energy'! **Keeping a level head is hard to do when you're the queen bee, but that's exactly what you must do.**

No matter how much better you feel your life is now that you've had all these incredible travel experiences, try to keep things in perspective. **Life is always a lesson in balance.** What goes up must come down and that applies to each of us. **Manage this new stage of your life as you would any other, with grace and humility, appreciation and a sense of gratitude.**

HUMBLE PIE IS ALWAYS SWEET

Be confident yet humble about your experiences. While you were out and about, traipsing around the globe, there were others holding the fort back home to keep things going. They must have been, otherwise how would you have such a nice soft landing pad to return to?

REMEMBER NOT TO TAKE FOR GRANTED WHAT YOU HAVE – EITHER AT HOME OR AWAY.

SHOW 'N' TELL

While we are on the subject about being humble, **it is always wise to downplay the amazing time you had when you were away. Being sensitive to others**, who may have been going through something difficult while you were having the time of your life, is sensible and shows you are mature. Don't brag or go on and on about your trip. People will ask if they are interested. **Showing off will put them off**.

Keep the mantra 'less is more' close! Don't assume they want to hear every single detail. Keep the trip photos to a minimum – pick out the top 20 and have something brief to say about each. Remember the golden rule of showbiz: **Always keep 'em wanting more**.

A BUMPY LANDING

Despite your best efforts to be positive about being home again, you may feel bogged down or are unable to get motivated about anything. As a result you may feel depressed. This is quite a normal response; however, if it becomes prolonged take action immediately. You may need to seek some counseling or visit your family doctor who can help you and monitor your moods.

We all feel down from time to time and coming home after being away can trigger a sense of being trapped. Maybe you have come back to a bunch of problems that you thought you'd 'escaped'. Old boyfriends, issues with your female friends or perhaps you resent living back with your parents (if you are). The independent time – your 'freedom' – that you may have enjoyed on your trip has come to an end for the time being. **This can produce a mix of emotions.**

GO EASY ON YOURSELF. IT TAKES TIME TO READJUST.

The best advice is to get a new plan and a new goal. You need to honor the feelings that you have – they are key indicators that a need you have must be met. So let that be your new challenge.

Above all, please talk to your parents, your friends, a counselor or a doctor. Don't shut everyone out or keep it to yourself. No matter what you think or what they think, if you communicate with them, everyone will understand. Truly.

RELATIONSHIP REVIEWS

No relationship stays the same. Like all things change is constant and relationships are subtly shifting all the time, as we do. If your relationships needed a review, the chances are you have had plenty of time to do that at 40,000 feet or while you crossed China in a train. So the current or ex-boyfriend may not fit into your 'Big Picture' anymore. Or you may feel that being in a small 'clique' of girlfriends doesn't work for you either.

Having seen how big the world is, you may have a burning desire to meet new people and make new friends, everywhere! The pie can get larger, which doesn't mean you have to dump anyone and it may not even be necessary to do so. Go ahead and review your relationships, but **be careful not to hurt anyone's feelings intentionally – act with compassion and honesty**.

BACK IN THE SADDLE: PLANNING THE NEXT ADVENTURE

If your daydreams of foreign landscapes are still haunting you after you return, then you will already know the signs: it's time to plan a new adventure! Refining your travel style is useful in planning your next trip. A quick review is helpful:

- WHAT WOULD YOU DO DIFFERENTLY next time?
- WHAT STUFF did you lug halfway around the world that YOU DIDN'T USE/NEED?
- WHAT TOOK UP FAR TOO MUCH SPACE?
- WHAT DIDN'T YOU TAKE that you actually needed?
- What would be on your 'MUST HAVE' LIST for next time?
- ALONE OR TOGETHER? What's your travel style?
- SHORTER OR LONGER? Did you need more/less time away?
- MONEY – how did you cope? Are you a spender or thrifty?
- Was your ACCOMMODATION too 'budget' for your comfort? Too expensive?

Reviewing all of these and any other questions you can think of regarding your trip will help you figure out how you travel best and what you personally need to do to plan for it properly. The knowledge you have gained and the things that work for you then become part of your travel plans for life.

MONEY ON THE REBOUND

Let's just pick up on that point about money. I mentioned earlier about the need to have some money for your return home. If you did spend your nest egg while you were away, you aren't alone. And while it might be very comfy lying on the couch at home eating chocolate or hanging out all the time at your friend's place watching DVDs, you simply can't do it forever!

You need to have a plan.
How will you pay for your mobile phone or outings? If you're out of cash and you're back home, that's a classic combination to make you feel pretty low, so avoid the dip and get busy ... now! It's the right time to get a new part-time or casual job. Volunteer to do babysitting, dog walking or odd jobs. **If you are trying to get a full-time job, get your resume in order and get out there with your best outfit on**.
Take massive action!

The sooner you regain your sense of independence and some sort of control over your finances, the better you will adapt to being home again.

CARPE DIEM! SEIZE THE DAY!

The hardest part of returning is feeling the 'old routine' settle around your shoulders. Everything that has been so colorful and different now seems a bit bland. But fear not, this feeling is usually only temporary. It doesn't mean you won't ever travel again or that life will never be as rich or as much fun as when you were away. Quite the contrary: you'll probably do more traveling now that you have had a taste. **Your recently expanded view of the world should have shown you**

THAT LIFE IS PRECIOUS AND SHORT,
AND WITH THIS CONSCIOUSNESS YOU SHOULD
SEIZE THE DAY!

The completion of a journey can be the beginning of something else. **Try not to see it as an ending; rather, view it as the dawn of a new age for yourself.** Creating a new routine so that life feels fresh again should be your number one focus. There is no sense moping about how much fun you had while you were away, you should still have a positive attitude. Let's face it: life can't always be fun, all of the time. But, **don't complain about how boring life is at home. If you think it's boring, think again. It might be (shock, horror) just ... you!**

Treat being at home in the same spirit that you treated the other countries and places you visited. Everywhere has something amazing to offer. Join up for the gym, a new yoga class, perhaps offer to walk dogs locally and get fit while you earn cash for your next travel adventure! Visit art galleries, see films and read new books. Catch up for show 'n' tell of your photos with your friends. Put a scrap book or photo album together with your travel diary notes and create a beautiful keepsake. There will be heaps to do – try making a list and surprise yourself!

> The time after a trip is the perfect opportunity to set some new goals for your life.

A trip away is always a prime opportunity to turn over a new leaf. **Reinvention is powerful** and it is best applied at a distance for maximum impact on re-entry! If you have radically changed while you were away – and this is a physical and mental change that can be readily observed by all who know you – then you may have to adjust to the fact that everyone else has to adjust to you too!

Be patient with those who are around you. Not only have you been away for a while, you're growing and developing in new ways and this is often hard for others to understand. You may have been to places they themselves have only ever heard of, and this may make them feel insecure or inadequate. They may feel – as a result of long absence and long distance – that they have somehow 'lost' you a bit or that you've outgrown them. **Reassure them that regardless of where you have been, you still respect and care for them**.

> # THE
> # JOURNEY,
> ## NOT
> # THE
> # ARRIVAL MATTERS.
>
> T. S. ELLIOT

BE HERE NOW

The best advice I ever had was from a friend who is an international flight attendant, many air miles and countless countries resulted in her rather simple philosophy: **'Wherever you go, there you are'**. This was a little obscure to me at one time but as the years have passed what meant has become clear: need to be where you are. can't spend your time wish you were somewhere el If you stay where you we you'll miss something wh you are. You are neither h nor there!

" E V E N THOUGH **IT MAY** BE THE LAST THING Y O U FEEL LIKE, YOU HAVE TO BE **HERE NOW.** "

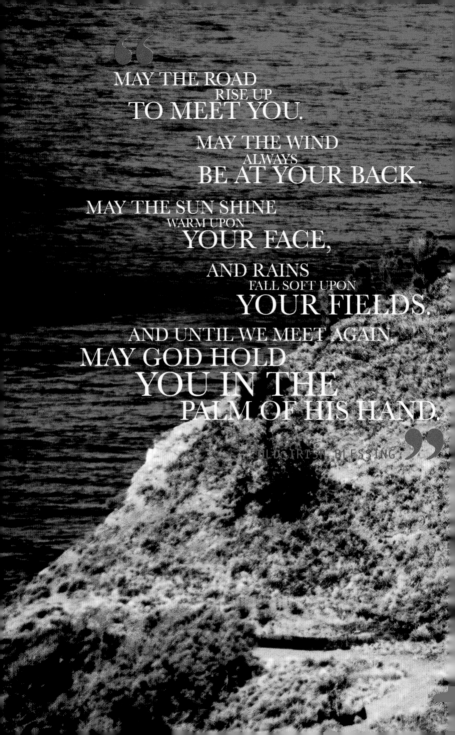
"MAY THE ROAD
RISE UP
TO MEET YOU.

MAY THE WIND
ALWAYS
BE AT YOUR BACK.

MAY THE SUN SHINE
WARM UPON
YOUR FACE,

AND RAINS
FALL SOFT UPON
YOUR FIELDS.

AND UNTIL WE MEET AGAIN,
MAY GOD HOLD
YOU IN THE
PALM OF HIS HAND.

OLD IRISH BLESSING"

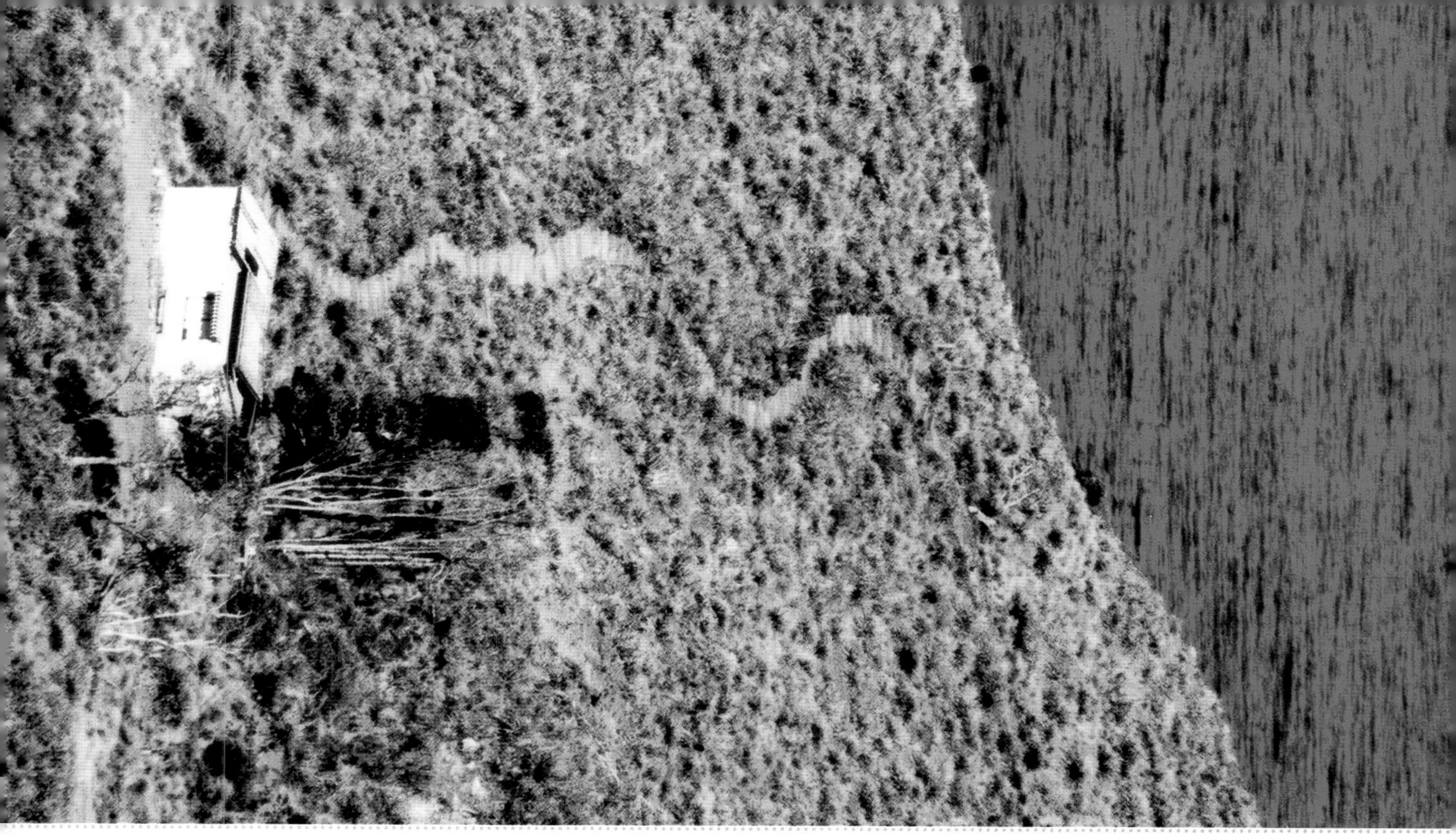

TRAVELING WITH THE WORLD WIDE WEB

WEBSITES TO SURF BEFORE YOU GO OUT THERE!

For more 'organic traveling' - especially if you are the type to change your mind at the last minute or if you decide to go to a new country on a whim - the net is the ultimate tool. Luckily for all of us, the now not-so-new kid on the block - the information superhighway - really comes into its own, putting the world of travel squarely in your hands. It's a wild, wide and wonderful world out there in www-ville. Stories, blogs, personal recommendations, photographs - so much more information about destinations than we have ever had in the past - are all available. For those who truly love to fly check out Google Earth and look at your destination before you arrive, such as the hotel you've booked and its nearest beach, internet café, ski resort, movie theater, etc., all in 3-D.

The information about the websites below is correct at the time we went to print; however please note that these can and do change often. As a precaution, please check websites are still live and current or at least regularly updated before you go, especially if you are planning on using them while you are away.

Also please note that some of these sites are US-based so if you are doing bookings or costings online please be careful with the rate of exchange. You should double-check and note all prices as you go so you don't get any nasty surprises.

HOT GIRLO TIP

• Read some of the blogs at My Trip Journal. You'll be amazed and amused at where some people end up and what they do once they get there. You can also sign up as a registered traveler at IgoUgo. Make friends and read the profiles of those adventurous souls who love to travel. (I spent days doing this!)

• Booking online is the most common use of the net but general browsing can really fire the imagination and get you thinking about places that may not even be on your radar yet. Surf the net before you even choose a destination or prepare an itinerary and you may end up with a completely new set of travel plans.

• One way to ensure you have the info you need is to forward a bunch of website links directly to your hotmail or other email account so you can access them more easily while you're away (and keep browsing time at internet cafés to a minimum thus saving your money).

• Photocopy or print out the relevant pages from online and guidebook sources. Bind them together in a small file that you keep in your hand luggage.

• Consulate information is best checked on websites first as they tend to keep unusual hours and/or close on public holidays that you may not be aware of. Particularly useful for travel warnings, breaking news and local weather information that may affect travelers to a region.

HEALTH

www.traveldoctor.com.au

This site is a terrific resource for when you are in the planning stages of a trip but also while you're away. This is an Australian site but it contains newsletters and regular updates on health issues in specific international locations and destinations, so it is a good resource no matter what country you're traveling from. The Travel Doctor TMVC recommends vaccinations and other essential health information to ensure your dream trip does not become a health nightmare. In addition, their medical kit is brilliant and comes with a handy reference booklet for the symptoms of many illnesses. I never leave home without it.

www.who.int/en

The World Health Organization has a comprehensive international health and travel publication which is updated yearly as a book and has the most up-to-date health information for when you're on the road. The 2007 edition was still in the process of being

GENERAL

www.gridskipper.com

This is a funky salon-style 'urban' travel site for those who want a fun and sometimes frivolous look at the world. <www.coolhunting.com> calls it 'decadence on a budget'. Gotta love it!

www.johnnyjet.com

This site claims to be the site where 'travel experts share their tips and expertise to make you the expert'. The travel portal has all the online links you could ever want – making johnnyjet an essential 'go to' resource. Plus, you have to hand it to a guy whose idea of the best use for his air miles is taking his mother to Europe!

www.concierge.com

Sigh. I get serious travel lust when I visit this site. Not just for the expensive destinations, although you can certainly find these. One of the features I found here had budget beach holidays in Mexico, St. Barths, Thailand, The Bahamas, Costa Rica, the Florida Keys and the Virgin Islands (just for starters). And

then click on [free translation]. It's a useful tool if want to look and act like a local. It may even get you better prices at the market!

www.IgoUgo.com

This site bills itself as presenting 'honest advice to get you going, travel reviews you can trust', while promising 'recommendations from other travelers. See the real people behind the advice. Share your own reviews and photos to earn rewards.' What's not to like?

www.sciencemadesimple.com

Convert anything on this site: currency, temperatures, distances, etc. Really useful.

GROUP TOURS

www.intrepidtravel.com

Group or individual packages to a good variety of destinations, targeting young people who prefer to travel in groups and who want to travel to an (exhausting!) array of exciting/exotic destinations

with an eco-friendly vibe with young but experienced guides. Intrepid has created the Intrepid Foundation to give back to the communities they tour and they also have a Responsible Tourism code or ethics, favoring community-based, grassroots travel options.

completed as at the time of going to print, however specific chapters are available online in PDF format which makes it easier if you need it while you're away.

www.cdc.gov

The official website for the Centers for Disease Control and Prevention (US), offers up-to-date information on vaccinations and immunizations plus general medical and health FAQs. This is a great search mechanism which offers variety and a comprehensive overview.

www.BasecampMD.com

Go where the mountaineering pros go! Log on to the medical clinic that is operated from the base of Mount Everest. Great information on altitude sickness, general trekking and climbing factoids, plus essential medical kit items are listed.

they let you know they're serious about the yuppy-vibe-with-hippy costs: coconut drinks on the beach at Phi Phi Island for US$2, sea salt scrub massages in Puerto Vallarta for US$55 and horse riding on the beach in Mozambique for US$25 to give you but a few incentives.

www.globorati.com

This site describes itself as 'jetset intelligence'. For most of us this is truly the stuff of daydreams. But it's sometimes worth knowing where the ultimate destinations are so you can stay down the road for a lot less and drop in for a cup of tea instead.

www.tripadvisor.com

Amateur reviews from travelers. Some are frank. Some are extreme, but at least you'll get the lowdown on what a hotel or tourist attraction is actually like! Many subjects, discussion forums, read postings and follow itineraries and discover what will work for you.

www.freetranslation.com

Just a great way to get some key phrases quickly. Go online and prepare your requests in the window,

www.manifestasafaris.com

Promising to 'make girls out of women' this US-based group provides creative, surfing and golfing safaris for women. You must be accompanied by someone over 18 if you are not yet legal age and you must be at least 14 years of age to join the surfing safaris at Las Olas, but why not get your Mom, Aunt or big sister to go with you? What could be better than learning to surf in Mexico? Or learning to play golf or simply to create art?

www.wickedwomentravel.com

A women-only travel organization. For all ages and stages, this travel company will organize or customize trips depending on your needs. You can go alone, with a friend or with a group of your choosing. They had Vietnam bike tours and a house in Tuscany when I visited the site, so they do offer variety.

www.escapesafaris.com.au

A holistic 'girls only' travel company: learn to surf with Yallingup Surf Safaris, see the sights, ride horses, go sea kayaking, eat amazing food, meet indigenous women for secret women's business.

for volunteering and make your trip really worthwhile for someone else.

www.peruschallenge.com

Travel with purpose by helping small rural communities in Peru. Brush up on your Spanish while you interact with locals and children at schools that have been purpose-built and staffed by volunteers. Come home with a bursting photo album, new friends for life and a heart full of satisfaction.

www.awaitingangels.com

Girlosopher Simone King worked with street children as a volunteer with Awaiting Angels in Trujillo, Peru. The group organizes placements and programs for international volunteers to get involved in orphanages, with Street kids, in health care, teacher assistants and children with AIDS. Awaiting Angels has designed programs and activities to provide volunteers with rewarding and inspirational service experiences, as well as to provide the children in the projects with the much-needed love and attention that they deserve.

You will experience the fabled south west coast of Australia at its best on these tailor-made safaris in the Margaret River region.

www.explorersweb.com
www.basecampMD.com

The menu says it all: [everest] [K2] [oceans] [poles] [space] [tech] [weather] [statistics] [medical]. You too can be an explorer of the final frontiers of our planet. Billing itself as The Pioneers Checkpoint, this site is for Serious Outdoor Types who like to smash world distance records, scale incredible heights and the like. Or for those who like to watch ... and wonder why they do it. If you're having a bad moment when you're away, click on and find some poor sod who's trapped in an ice cave in a blizzard, or who is in the middle of the ocean with ominous fins circling their boat. Now you know someone is definitely having a worse day than you.

www.statravel.com.au

Good old Student Travel can always be relied upon to look for the cheapest and the best travel options. They also offer an impressive '500 projects in 27 countries' if you'd like to volunteer while you're away.

VOLUNTEERING

www.i-to-i.com

Life changing travel for real! Volunteering to contribute to a project in another country is a great way to travel. When I visited the site, there was an opportunity to work on a rural Uganda project and be part of a UK television documentary. People were also off to Kenya to volunteer, and yet another girl had just come back from a project in Argentina and was about to go to India (both of which she did when she was just 20). Discussion forums are interesting on this site and perhaps because of the type of people who volunteer they are also generous with their information and enthusiasm. Plenty of volunteering opportunities for teens but also scope for older people to participate. Restore your faith!

www.unitedplanet.org

Oscar-winning actor Hilary Swank became a volunteer for United Planet recently – she did a stint as a caregiver and teaching assistant in North India through their Volunteer Abroad Quest. You can do the same. Check out the testimonials and options

GUIDEBOOKS

www.lonelyplanet.com <.au (Aust);.fr (France);.co.uk (UK)>

The ubiquitous but evergreen series of travel books is a fantastic resource at home or away and also online. So much to read, so many places, so many postcards to send.

www.roughguides.com

The other guidebook source that is great for comparisons on destinations and reviews. Their US and Australia guidebooks are particularly good (and personally tested!).

www.fodors.com

More a Mom 'n' Dad guidebook version but they still have good reviews and are worth checking out for comparisons, especially for the major tourist destinations and attractions plus helpful transit/transport info. Nothing like another opinion!

www.wallpaper.com

The ultra-chic design magazine Wallpaper® doesn't (let's face it, you don't need to hook up with Crazy Guy/Girl, Needy Dude or Cheap Chick while you're away). But Wayn is a fun site, even if you're only browsing at home. You can also Save the Dolphins while you're here.

www.traveleor.com

This site is for those who want to create a personal website while they are away for long periods of time, as a way of keeping in touch. The site template is clear and easy to navigate. Not too much advertising means it feels more personal. I was fascinated with a young English couple, JJ and Chloe, who are working on an Eco-marine project in Malaysia.

www.notesfromtheroad.com

One of my favorite travel blogs. The site is gorgeous to look at: Eric's pictures are always dreamy and he writes beautifully about what's really going on in a variety of far-flung destinations. He also does his own superb pen and ink maps for each location. Sigh. Inspired travel, indeed.

www.virtualtourist.com

Another great travel blog site but which functions more like a community. One plus is that the photos the lower-end price range and they came back with a dizzying 355 choices. This site will change all the time so check listings carefully.

www.lastminute.com or www.lastminute.com.au

Always worth a look but sadly you can't always expect a bargain.

www.seatguru.com

Indispensable website for working out what seats to request once you know what plane you're getting. Better yet, give your travel or booking agent your preferred seating choices in every type of plane that (say) Qantas has, and never again worry that you'll get stuck in the aisle right next to the toilets after the movie finishes.

www.australia.com or www.italy.com or www.mexico.com you get the idea.

Usually the official government sites (well it is for Australia at least!). Search for all things travel-oriented in the country of your choice.

www.flightcentre.com.au www.priceline.com

disappoint with its online offerings – it's worth it just for the time zone clocks for Tokyo, New York, London and Sydney. The Wallpaper® Cities guides are also just the ticket – small and super smart (the full range is available through <www.phaidon.com/travel>).They're on the money but you'll have to be careful with yours especially if you're on a budget. Groovy Baby.

TRAVEL BLOGS

www.mytripjournal.com

The Personal Travel Website for bloggers. Read Adrian's hilarious Best & Worst of China List – it's exactly what real travel is like. Discover why Voodoo spread from Africa to Haiti. Find out what not to buy in Amsterdam. Share your trip and blog on while you're on the road, so everyone can tune in to where you're at (and turn pea green with envy).

www.wayn.com

Where Are You Now? Hook up with fellow travelers while you're on the road. Check the profiles but – as always – a word of caution: please be fussy

are pretty good and there are loads of posts.

BOOKINGS AND COSTINGS

www.iccfx.com/convert

Not having a handle on the real cost of items when you're in a foreign country is one of the biggest mistakes that travelers make. So it's best to get on top of how to convert your precious pennies while it's not costing you a fortune to learn! This site has a simple converter and is a good place to practice using your calculator before you go away. The rates may vary slightly once you get there, but if you check before you leave, at least you'll have some idea of what to expect. You do the math!

www.kayak.com

This site is a filtering system that gives users an amazing array of choice. For any budget, it will provide options and is simple to use. I tested it by requesting Buenos Aires hotels with no stars and in

www.skoosh.com
www.travelzoo.com
www.breezenet.com

These sites are great for discount flights and up-to-the minute bargain specials – big picture pricing to destinations (but not necessarily always the cheapest). Check and recheck!

TRIP PLANNER / ITINERARY

The following page can be photocopied and added to your file to take with you on the plane with all your ticketing / insurance papers / passport etc. Update the information for each leg of the journey and that way you'll have a quick 'Go-To' check list for what you need / when you need it.

Be careful to copy across the information carefully from original source documents. Double check all dates and times. If you're nervous, do have someone else check it as well just to make sure you didn't make any mistakes.

"Give a copy to your loved ones and friends so they can track your progress and stay in touch.

Bon Voyage!"

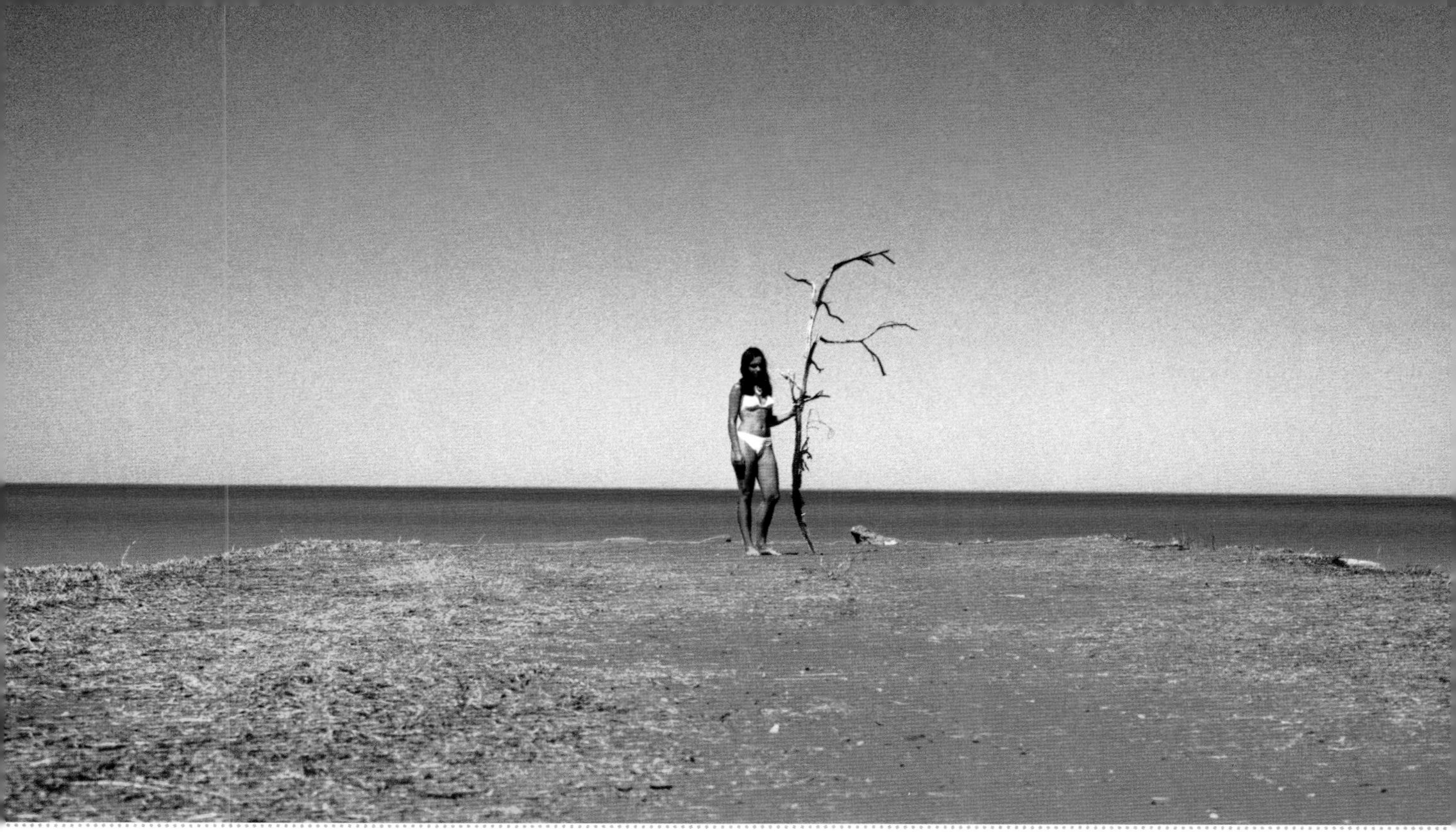

PERSONAL INFORMATION:

NAME

DATE OF BIRTH

ADDRESS

PHONE NUMBERS

HOME   MOBILE

EMAIL ADDRESS / BLOG PASSWORD ETC

CITIZENSHIP   PASSPORT NUMBER

EMERGENCEY CONTACT DETAILS:

NAME

ADDRESS

PHONE NUMBERS

HOME   MOBILE

OTHER DESTINATION INFORMATION:

EMBASSY PHONE NUMBERS:

ACCOMMODATION DETAILS:

ADDRESS

PHONE NUMBER

WEBSITE

FRIEND'S DETAILS:

NAME

ADDRESS

PHONE NUMBERS

HOME   MOBILE

WEBSITES:

TRIP DETAILS:

DESTINATION 1
DEPARTING FROM

DATE .... TIME ....

ARRIVING TO

DATE .... TIME ....

DESTINATION 2
DEPARTING FROM

DATE .... TIME ....

ARRIVING TO

DATE .... TIME ....

DESTINATION 3
DEPARTING FROM

DATE .... TIME ....

ARRIVING TO

DATE .... TIME ....

DESTINATION 4
DEPARTING FROM

DATE .... TIME ....

ARRIVING TO

DATE .... TIME ....

CURRENCY EXCHANGE:

COUNTRY

DATE .... RATE ....

COUNTRY

DATE .... RATE ....

COUNTRY

DATE .... RATE ....

COUNTRY

DATE .... RATE ....

ROUGH PLANS / PLACES OF INTEREST:

OTHER DETAILS:

INDEX

CHILDREN
NORTHERN SRI LANKA

WHEN YOU TRAVEL, REMEMBER THE CHILDREN.

VISIT WWW.UNICEF.ORG TO SEE HOW YOU CAN
HELP ONCE YOU GET HOME.

THE UNITED NATIONS CHILDREN'S FUND (UNICEF).

ANTHEA PAUL

Anthea Paul is the author of the bestselling and award-winning girlosophy series of books. She has worked internationally as a stylist, photo editor and art director in the fashion, design and publishing industries.

A nomadic photographer and writer, Anthea contributes to a variety of women's and surfing magazines internationally. Based on the northern beaches of Sydney, Australia, Anthea is also a proud supporter of the charity War Child International and of The Tibetan Friendship group (TFG).

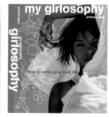

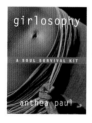

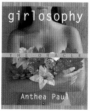
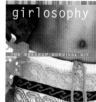

www.girlosophy.com